A Meatloaf
in
Every Oven

ALSO BY FRANK BRUNI

Where You Go Is Not Who You'll Be

Born Round

Ambling into History

ALSO BY JENNIFER STEINHAUER

Treat Yourself

Beverly Hills *Adjacent* (with Jessica Hendra)

A Meatloaf in Every Oven

Two Chatty Cooks,

One Iconic Dish and

Dozens of Recipes—

from Mom's to Mario Batali's

Frank Bruni & Jennifer Steinhauer

ILLUSTRATIONS BY

MARILYN POLLACK NARON

GRAND CENTRAL
Life & Style
NEW YORK · BOSTON

Grand Central Life & Style
Hachette Book Group
1290 Avenue of the Americas, New York, NY 10104
grandcentrallifeandstyle.com
twitter.com/grandcentralpub

First Edition: February 2017

Grand Central Life & Style is an imprint of Grand Central Publishing. The Grand Central Life & Style name and logo are trademarks of Hachette Book Group, Inc.
The publisher is not responsible for websites (or their content) that are not owned by the publisher.
The Hachette Speakers Bureau provides a wide range of authors for speaking events. To find out more, go to www.hachettespeakersbureau.com or call (866) 376-6591.

"A Meatless Loaf for Dennis" courtesy of Cathy Barrow • "Mario Batali's Stuffed Meatloaf" courtesy of Mario Batali • "April Bloomfield's Lamb Loaf with Yogurt and Mint" courtesy of April Bloomfield • "Melissa Clark's Salmon Loaf with Mustard and Capers" courtesy of Melissa Clark • "Senator Susan Collins's Bipartisan Loaf" courtesy of Susan Collins • "Helene's Extremely Delicious Mashed Potatoes" courtesy of Helene Cooper • "Bobby Flay's Korean-Style Meatloaf with Spicy Glaze" and "Bobby Flay's Shiitake Mushroom Salad" courtesy of Bobby Flay • "Garret Fleming's Macaroni and Cheese" courtesy of Garret Fleming • "Joan Futter's Meatloaf" courtesy of Deb Futter • "Alex Guarnaschelli's Mom's Meatloaf" courtesy of Alex Guarnaschelli • "Amanda Hesser's Couscous with Celery, Parsley and Red Wine Vinegar" courtesy of Amanda Hesser • "'It's Maaaa-gic!' Moroccan Carrots" courtesy of Virginia Kellner • "Meatloaf with Moroccan Flair" courtesy of Anne Kornblut • "Spicy Turkey Loaf with Sriracha" courtesy of Erin McDowell • "Annie Miler's Home-Style Loaf with Cheddar and Parsley" courtesy of Annie Miler • "Sam Molavi's Wow Brussels Sprouts" courtesy of Sam Molavi • "Daniel Patterson's Zucchini Loaf" courtesy of Daniel Patterson • "Nancy Pelosi's Italian-Style Bison Loaf" courtesy of Nancy Pelosi • "Oh Deer, Speaker Paul Ryan's Loaf" courtesy of Paul Ryan • "Senator Chuck Schumer's Omnibus Loaf" courtesy of Chuck Schumer • "Michael Schwartz's Kasha Loaf with Caramelized Onion Gravy" courtesy of Michael Schwartz • "Winter Salad of Fennel, Celery Root, Lemon and Pecorino" courtesy of Cristina Sciarra • "Mike Solomonov's Spicy Merguez Loaf" courtesy of Mike Solomonov • "Tuna Loaf Glazed with Mushrooms and Red Wine" courtesy of Mark Usewicz • "Volpe Family Loaf with Ham" courtesy of Paul Volpe • "Michael White's Chicken Eggplant Loaf" courtesy of Michael White

Illustrations: Marilyn Pollack Naron

Library of Congress Cataloging-in-Publication Data

Names: Bruni, Frank, author. | Steinhauer, Jennifer, author. | Naron, Marilyn Pollack, illustrator.
Title: A meatloaf in every oven : two chatty cooks, one iconic dish and dozens of recipes-from Mom's to Mario Batali's / by Frank Bruni and Jennifer Steinhauer ; illustrations by Marilyn Pollack Naron.
Description: New York : GCP Life & Style, [2017] | Includes index.
Identifiers: LCCN 2016025917| ISBN 9781455563050 (hardcover) | ISBN 9781455563067 (ebook)
Subjects: LCSH: Meat loaf. | LCGFT: Cookbooks.
Classification: LCC TX749 .B83 2017 | DDC 641.82/4—dc23 LC record available at https://lccn.loc.gov/2016025917

ISBNs: 978-1-4555-6305-0 (hardcover), 978-1-4555-6306-7 (ebook)

Book design by Fearn Cutler de Vicq
Printed in the United States of America
LSC-C
10 9 8 7 6 5 4 3 2 1

Contents

Contents

In loving memory of Nora Ephron,

who relished meatloaf as much as she did life—

and who showed the two of us the beauty (and comedy) in each

Contributors

(in alphabetical order)

Cathy Barrow

Cathy, the author of the food blog *Mrs. Wheelbarrow's Kitchen*, is a canning and cooking teacher and food preservation expert. She writes the "DIY" column in the *Washington Post*'s Food section and a quarterly column for *Allrecipes* magazine. She has also written for NPR and for the *New York Times*, *Garden and Gun*, *Saveur*, *Southern Living* and *National Geographic*, among other publications. In 2015, she won the prestigious IACP Award for best single-subject cookbook for *Mrs. Wheelbarrow's Practical Pantry*.

Mario Batali

With his red hair, his orange clogs and his passion for all things Italian, Mario has become one of the best known and most beloved American chefs of the last quarter century. He owns twenty-six restaurants around the world, including, most recently, La Sirena, in New York City, the center of his culinary empire. He's also an educator, the author of eleven cookbooks (the most recent of which is *Big American Cookbook*) and a host of the ABC daytime talk show *The Chew*.

April Bloomfield

April, who was trained in Britain, shot to culinary fame in the United States with the 2003 opening of the gastropub The Spotted Pig in Manhattan's West Village. Both that restaurant and another Manhattan one, The Breslin, earned Michelin stars, making April one of a select group of New York chefs with multiple Michelin-starred places. She's also a chef-owner of the Manhattan restaurants The John Dory and Salvation Burger. She's the author of the cookbook *A Girl and Her Greens: Hearty Meals from the Garden*.

Melissa Clark

Melissa is a writer for the Food section of the *New York Times*, where her popular column "A Good Appetite" regularly appears. She has also written thirty-eight cookbooks, many of them in collaboration with some of New York's most celebrated chefs, including Daniel Boulud (*Braise*), Andrew Feinberg (*Franny's*), Claudia Fleming (*The Last Course*) and White House pastry chef Bill Yosses (*The Perfect Finish*). Her next cookbook, *Dinner*, a guide to taking nightly meals to the next level, will be published by Clarkson Potter in 2017.

Bobby Flay

Bobby is one of the shining stars of the Food Network and has been showcased in more than a half dozen of its cooking shows over the last decade, including the current hit *Beat Bobby Flay*. His restaurants span the globe, and his chain *Bobby's Burger Palace* sprawls over a dozen states. But he remains especially proud of his two acclaimed Manhattan restaurants: Bar Americain, which reflects his long romance with Southwestern cooking, and Gato, which demonstrates his fluency in Spanish cuisine.

Garret Fleming

Garret was a contestant in Season 13 of *Top Chef* and is, in fact, the top chef at Barrel, a restaurant in Washington, D.C., that specializes in bourbon in the glass and Southern cooking on the plate, which Garret honed in his native Charleston, South Carolina, at the Peninsula Grill and Mercato. He was one of the brains behind the popular Washington restaurants Lincoln and The Pig before bringing his talents to the kitchen at Barrel in 2014.

Alex Guarnaschelli

Alex's busy career spans TV shows on the Food Network and the Cooking Channel; a book, *Old-School Comfort Food: The Way I Learned to Cook,* that combines recipes with autobiographical reflections; and the Manhattan restaurant Butter, where she's the executive chef. She became only the second woman ever to be crowned "America's Next Iron Chef" when she received that honor on *Iron Chef America* in 2012.

Amanda Hesser

Author of the best seller *The Essential New York Times Cookbook,* Amanda was a *New York Times* food scribe for several years before breaking out to co-found Food52.com, the groundbreaking (and award-winning) site where cooks exchange recipes, ideas and kitchen tips. She is also the author of *Cooking for Mr. Latte: A Food Lover's Courtship, with Recipes* and *The Cook and the Gardener.* In Nora Ephron's feature film *Julie & Julia,* an homage to Julia Child, Amanda played herself.

Annie Miler

Annie trained at the Cordon Bleu in London and in several Los Angeles restaurants, including Campanile and Spago Beverly Hills. But she learned to make her trademark celestial baked goods from her grand-mother in the Midwest and her comfort food at cult-favorite Clementine, which she opened in Century City in 2000. A Beverly Hills branch came along in 2012.

Sam Molavi

Compass Rose, in Washington, D.C., is where Sam got his first gig as executive chef, drawing on his knowledge of the global ingredients that form the restaurant's menu. His culinary education is decidedly old-school: His father was a chef in the District, and his mother manages one of its premier groceries. He is the former sous-chef at Ripple, also in the District.

Daniel Patterson

Daniel, a California chef, writer and restaurateur, was named "Best Chef: West" in 2014 by the James Beard Foundation. At twenty-five he opened his first restaurant, Babette's, in Sonoma, and he has since built a small California empire. His restaurant group, DPG, oversees Coi (which propelled the cookbook *Coi: Stories and Recipes*), Alta CA and Aster in San Francisco and Plum Bar + Restaurant and Haven in Oakland. He recently started a wholesome fast-food chain, LocoL, with Los Angeles chef Roy Choi.

Michael Schwartz

A winner of the James Beard Award and all manner of other ac-claim, Michael first made his national mark with the opening in 2006 of Michael's Genuine Food & Drink in the Miami Design District, a neighborhood that his restaurant helped to put on the map. His subsequent South Florida restaurants, all part of the Genuine Hospitality Group, include Harry's Pizzeria, Cypress Tavern and ella. He is also the author, with JoAnn Cianciulli, of *Michael's Genuine Food: Down-to-Earth Cooking for People Who Love to Eat*, which showcases recipes from the Michael's Genuine restaurant, still going strong.

Mike Solomonov

Mike is considered the foremost American advocate of what he describes as modern Israeli cuisine, which is the focus of his internationally renowned restaurant, Zahav, in Philadelphia. His 2015 book, *Zahav: A World of Israeli Cooking*, written with Steven Cook, was an instant best seller. His other Philadelphia restaurants include Abe Fisher, Dizengoff, Rooster Soup Co. and several locations of Federal Donuts. He branched out to Manhattan with Dizengoff NYC. He's also the star of the PBS documentary *In Search of Israeli Cuisine*.

Mark Usewicz

Mark's obsession with opening a fish market was sparked by his wife, a scientist with a background in marine biology. His culinary education began in Paris, wove its way through Boston and landed him in Brooklyn, where he co-founded Mermaid's Garden, a fish shop, restaurant and consultancy.

Michael White

Michael is one of the country's most venerated interpreters of Italian cuisine, the various byways of which he explores at his hugely popular

New York restaurants, including Marea, which is devoted to Italian sea-food, and Osteria Morini, which explores the Emilia-Romagna region. He's also the head chef and part owner of the Altamarea Group, which operates more than a dozen restaurants internationally, in locations as far-flung as London, Istanbul and Hong Kong.

A Meatloaf in Every Oven

Introduction

Once upon a meatloaf, two perpetually busy, uncommonly hungry *New York Times* writers discovered that they shared a kitchen passion.

They were talking about eating, which was a favorite sport of theirs. They were talking about cooking, which they did at disparate skill levels. One of the writers, a woman, was as fearless at the stove as she was at City Hall, where she routinely grilled the mayor. She could whip up practical meals for her picky kids one minute and impractical feasts for sophisticated friends the next. The other writer, a man, was once the newspaper's chief restaurant critic and knew his way around a dozen ethnic cuisines, but he was shy with a spatula, timid with tongs and all nerves in front of the food processor. To pulse or not to pulse? He could stand there for an hour, dithering instead of dicing.

"Is there any dish that you feel confident about?" she asked him.

"Just one," he confided. But then he paused, because he was sure that what he was about to divulge would shame him. Few if any of the restaurants he appraised had it on their menus.

"You can tell me," she said.

He apologized that the dish wasn't fancy.

He apologized that it wasn't some farm-to-table wonder, dependent on the seasons, resplendent with obscure vegetables.

He apologized that he was apologizing.

And then he talked about ground chuck, tomato sauce, Worcestershire sauce, brown sugar and how his mother mingled these in an entree that was the quintessence of comfort, at least if comfort includes bread crumbs.

He talked about an analogue to it that he'd more or less invented, comprising ground lamb, feta, fresh mint and more.

He talked about mixing these with his hands and molding them with his fingers.

"Meatloaf," he said. "I make meatloaf."

She didn't flinch. She didn't sneer. She beamed, nodding so fast and hard that he feared for her neck. Almost instantly, they began discussing the sturdy virtues of ground pork. They moved on to the debatable utility of ground veal. And ground turkey: Was it truly viable, or was it the great white whale of meatloaves?

The next thing they knew—the next thing *we* knew—we were in meatloaf love.

So consider this book a love story, written in the special language of our relationship, with its vocabulary of ounces and tablespoons, of lightly beaten eggs and coarsely grated cheese, of cayenne pepper and smoked paprika. It reflects a decade's worth of weekly and sometimes daily conversations distinguished by abrupt topic shifts and abundant non-sequiturs. On the phone, we'll do fifteen minutes of office gossip ("I hear they're yanking him from Europe") followed abruptly by five minutes on meatloaf moistening ("Have you tried soaking the bread in whole milk?"). In a given series of e-mails, we'll toggle from Senate filibusters to sautéed shiitakes, from Obamacare to oregano. Always we snap back to meatloaf. It's our default setting. It's our North Star. We've exchanged recipes for it by text, by instant messenger, by Google chat.

We've also exchanged recipes with colleagues, friends and celebrated chefs, many of whom—including Mario Batali, Bobby Flay, April Bloomfield and Alex Guarnaschelli—shared their favorites with us for inclusion in this book. And we have discovered in the process that everybody has his or her own meatloaf story, meatloaf sensibility, meatloaf biases. Meatloaf is the most personal of dishes, and the most autobiographical. Show us a person's meatloaf and we'll show you that person's soul. Meatloaf is mirror: You are how you loaf.

Meatloaf is metaphor: It's life made loaf. You take what's precious (in this case, the meat) and stretch it as far as it'll go. And you learn that there are infinite ways to do this, an embarrassment of options. You need only flex your imagination. You need only raid the cupboard. Do you bring in the exotic? Incorporate some fire? Meatloaf is a yardstick for your daring, a referendum on your imagination, a judge of your loyalty to precedent, an arbiter of your regard for the classics.

Just as you can paper over your own flaws and smooth out your own shortcomings, you can redeem your meatloaf with split-second inspiration, last-minute epiphanies. You can improvise. You can adjust.

Is the meat mixture you're about to mold too weepy? Bread crumbs are your emotional caulk. Too dry? Another egg is your calmative. Bland? That's why the universe created hot sauce, and that's why it created so many of them: Tabasco, Sriracha, salsa picante. They speak in different dialects. They make different meatloaves. And when all else fails, add bacon. This is true in life, and this is true in loaf.

Meatloaf is spontaneity itself, and more than any other dish, it brings out the kid in the adult, repurposing child's play as mature, purposeful activity. Did you ever have one of those at-home chemistry sets with different liquids and different powders that you could combine in countless ways, for countless hues? Meatloaf is its kitchen cousin. Ever burrowed your fingers into Play-Doh? Meatloaf is its kin, best sculpted with bare hands. It's mischief made protein. It's fun that actually feeds.

It's as forgiving as a laid-back god. One egg or two? This matters less than you might think. A few dashes too much vinegar? The Earth will continue spinning, and your meatloaf will be just fine. You needn't be as punctilious with your measuring cups and spoons as you are when making pastry. You can guesstimate. You can round. It's all being absorbed into something greater, all going into the oven and will all work itself out.

There's not a recipe among the dozens here that you should feel exactingly yoked to and irrevocably bound by. Don't mess with the fundamental ratios of meat to its binders and moisteners. Don't take extravagant liberties with the cooking times. Don't get glaze-happy and wind up with soup. But otherwise, you can dial up the spices if that's your druthers, swap out bread crumbs for crackers if you're feeling the itch. We can't promise a result that'll be as wholly pleasing as the one you'll achieve with recipe fidelity, but we can predict that you'll wind up with something sufficiently satisfying—and all your own.

Because meatloaf is customizable. It allows for a personal stamp. It can be ambitious or humble, its flexibility demonstrated by its ability to bridge the two of us and by this book's recipes, most of them easily mastered but a few of them more challenging and time-consuming. You can dress meatloaf up or you can dress it down. You can treat it like royalty or treat it like a ragamuffin. We go in both directions, allowing it to experiment with eclectic costumes and an array of accents. We turn it into the Meryl Streep of comfort food.

*　　*　　*

That's not hard to do, because the meatloaf tradition is a global one. You find meatloaf on just about every continent (we're hedging here, because we can't swear to Antarctica) and in scores of countries, at least if you acknowledge, for example, that a meatball is to a meatloaf as a sapling is to a tree: It just hasn't grown and realized its full potential. In that sense Middle Eastern kibbeh (or kibbe or kebbah, depending on the region) is related to meatloaf, an example of the impulse to grind meat and then extend and amplify it in ways that also bind it into a shape that holds together. Kibbe are balls, tiny torpedoes or even patties of, typically, ground lamb or ground beef with minced onions, cracked wheat, maybe sautéed pine nuts and various spices. What does that resemble? A meatloaf.

And what's a fine French pâté or terrine, really, but a meatloaf in shrunken, silken, delicate drag? It starts with meat and puts it through a drill fundamentally similar to the grinding, binding and seasoning that lead to meatloaf. In their book *Charcuterie*, Michael Ruhlman and Brian Polcyn refer to pâté as "the Cinderella meat loaf," by which they mean the young woman in a ball gown before midnight, not the sooty chimney sweeper of the morning after. A meatloaf is a pâté minus its glass slippers.

Meatloaf in its larger, truer form exists in Vietnam, where it's boiled and called *gio*. It exists in South Africa, where it's animated by curry (and, sometimes, dried fruit) and called *bobotie*. Chileans often put hard-boiled eggs in their meatloaves. So do Italians and Germans. Meatloaf enjoys particular popularity in Scandinavia and other parts of northern Europe, including Sweden; there are culinary anthropologists who see a link between the modern meatloaf and the Swedish meatball. What you're snacking on at IKEA isn't merely a post-shopping canapé. It's a miniature meatloaf.

But where did it all begin? How far into the past must we travel to see, on the culinary horizon, the meatloaf lumbering into view?

There are various theories. There are competing histories, including the belief that meatloaf, or its closest antecedent, emerged in medieval Europe, around the fifth century, in a Mediterranean dish of finely diced meat scraps joined with fruits, nuts and seasonings. From that moment on, meatloaf in its many iterations and guises was often a sort of culinary scrap heap, a refuge for leftovers, in the spirit of many casseroles and of shepherd's pie. It was a way to stretch protein. It was a way to use up excess vegetables. It was a ragtag orchestra of ingredients on the verge of expiration. And it made music more uplifting than anyone could have anticipated.

Americans embraced it with more fondness and fervor than perhaps anyone else, to a point where it's often mentioned alongside hot dogs and hamburgers as one of the country's iconic dishes and essential comfort foods. Its narrative in this country includes an early chapter set in colonial times, when German immigrants made scrapple, an amalgam of ground pork and cornmeal that established the meat-starch union at the core of most meatloaves.

The first recorded recipe for the modern American meatloaf is from the late 1870s, according to the food historian Andrew Smith, who told us that it instructed the cook to finely chop "whatever cold meat you have." That meat, he said, would likely be beef, because New Englanders killed their cows before winter, when feeding them would prove more difficult, and

tried to take full advantage of every last bit of the meat, looking for uses for the cheap cuts. Meatloaf was such a use. To the chopped beef they added pepper, salt, onion, slices of milk-soaked bread and egg. You'll find these very ingredients and steps in many a meatloaf recipe today. But back then, Smith said, meatloaf wasn't for dinner. It was for breakfast.

From the late 1800s, a meatloaf-esque recipe for ground veal with bread crumbs and eggs appeared in the Boston Cooking-School Cook Book. But the profile of meatloaf rose to a whole new level in the 1890s, with the spread of industrial-scale meatpacking, which created scraps aplenty. Scraps were best chopped or ground and softened and seasoned, and that's precisely what happened to them in a burger, in a meatball and in the most physically imposing member of this culinary family: the meatloaf. The meatloaf was a home not just for scraps but for spices that connected it to the cook's epicurean ancestry. One old American recipe combined veal, ham and bread crumbs with grated nutmeg, mace, cayenne and lemon rind for a decidedly French flavor profile. This loaf was covered with an egg wash and crushed crackers.

Meatloaf became a staple of many Americans' diets during the Depression, because it helped home cooks extend precious protein farther than it might otherwise go, so that more people could be fed with less meat. By then meat grinders were common and meat grinding less difficult, two developments that helped to popularize meatloaf. In the 1940s meatloaf was an emblem of wartime ingenuity; this was the era of Penny Prudence's "Vitality Loaf," made with beef, pork and liver. The Culinary Arts Institute published a recipe for Savory Meat Loaf that called for beef, vegetable soup and cereal.

By the 1950s, meatloaf was here to stay. Betty Crocker had recipes, which home cooks tweaked. A 1958 book, 365 Ways to Cook Hamburger, included seventy recipes for meatloaf, and while you won't find nearly that many here, that's because some of those seventy went a bit wild, advocating smashed bananas, for example, or ketchup-filled peach halves. (We've exercised more restraint.) Meatloaf became an expected option at American diners. It never made inroads like that into upscale restaurants, but every now and then, an ambitious chef will sneak it onto his or her menu, either presenting it in some exalted form or keeping it simple and serving it as an act of nostalgia, as a gesture of respect for a food that so ably sustained Americans through hard times.

We both feel that when we cook meatloaf, we're connected to something bigger: a tradition, a time line. Meatloaf is elemental. It's enduring. And if comfort foods are those that are not only an answer to hunger but also an existential balm, served without undue fuss or expensive implements, then meatloaf rules the category. It reigns supreme. It's the fluffy caftan of comfort foods.

* * *

And yet. Meatloaf can be as divisive and polarizing as American politics. There are meatloaf partisans who believe that the ultimate meatloaf harbors equal measures of ground beef, ground pork and ground veal, and there are others who feel that ground veal is a wanly flavored waste of time. There are people who "bloom" powdered gelatin in water and mix this into their meatloaf before putting it in the oven, as a sort of insurance policy against drying or disintegration, and there are others, like us, who think that too many extra steps almost ruin the point of meatloaf, which should never be a headache, and that good ingredients used in proper proportion should in most cases eliminate any need for gelatin.

We admit to our own meatloaf prejudices and we come to meatloaf with our subjective pointers, and it's time now to present these: our meat-loaf manifesto. We'll do that by going through the usual components and construction of meatloaf.

While we contend that all sorts of ground meats make for great meat-loaf, we caution you not to go too lean, because you'll end up with a dry meatloaf. Meatloaf is not a diet food, so don't try to bully it into being one. Meet and eat it on its own terms.

That said, we have recipes for meatless loaves in the pages to follow. A few are entirely vegetarian, while a few use fish. We also have a few turkey meatloaf recipes that are certainly lower in calories and fat than, for example, our Homely Homey Blue and Bacon Loaf, which is a splen-diferous nutritional apocalypse. (We won't pretend otherwise, and we make no apologies.) But we're more intent on moistness and flavor than on virtue. For a turkey or chicken meatloaf, we recommend dark meat over white. When buying ground beef, don't look for lean sirloin; fatty chuck will serve you better. One of the reasons that lamb works so well in meatloaves—and that we have several recipes calling for ground lamb—is because of its fat content. It produces a luscious loaf.

If you've used only traditional bread crumbs in your meatloaf, you haven't scratched the surface of starchy binders and of ways to incorporate bread. Many of our recipes specify bread soaked in milk or half-and-half, because that can add extra moisture to a loaf that either needs or would benefit from it. When we do use dried bread crumbs, we sometimes sug-gest panko, or Japanese bread crumbs, as they work beautifully in meat-loaf, having a fluffier effect. But the function of bread crumbs can also be achieved with oatmeal, with farro, with crushed saltines, with cooked rice, even with cornflakes: We've seen and tried recipes with all of these possibilities and more. One of the recipes that made the book's final cut ditches bread crumbs in favor of tortilla chips; another assigns the role to potato chips.

We tend to lean away from raw onions—and most other raw vegetables—and generally instruct you to sauté them in either olive oil or butter, depending on the recipe. Doing this takes the over-aggressive bite out of onions and can prevent chopped vegetables from turning your meatloaf gritty. It's a textural upgrade.

Use your food processor discerningly. It's always tempting to reduce work and save time by putting onions, carrots, celery and such in the food processor instead of chopping them by hand, but if you do that, make sure not to reduce those vegetables to a paste, as that's not always the best form and consistency for them if they're going into a loaf, which is supposed to have a certain variation, a certain unevenness and even dots of color. Pulse a bit, then check the vegetables, then pulse a bit more. Repeat that until they're diced well but not to a fare-thee-well. Or do the work with a *sharpened* knife. Sometimes chopping feels like grueling work because you're doing it with a bad knife whose edge has dulled.

Our caveat about food processors is related to another bit of advice: Don't get so carried away with the mixing of your meatloaf that you over-work it, striving for some kind of immaculate blend. That's not meatloaf's nature. That's not its calling. Its wrinkles and blemishes are essential to its homespun, earthbound charms, and a pasty uniformity in a meatloaf is like an excess of Botox and filler on a face. It elevates flawlessness over character and creates something suspicious, strange and less inviting than arresting.

Use your hands with abandon. There are meatloaf recipes that will tell you to mix the ground meat and everything else with a spoon, but you'd need some kind of magical spoon and some kind of magical strength for that approach to be nearly as efficient and effective as rolling up your sleeves and treating the mixture the way you would treat dough in the bread-making process. Just be sure to wash your hands well beforehand, and take the meat out of the refrigerator a good twenty to thirty minutes before you're going to need (and knead) it, so it's not so cold that the work is actually unpleasant. The meat will also loosen up and mix better if it's at room temperature. Have the skillet or pan in which you're going to place the mixture nearby, because your hands will be sticky and clumpy, and you want to limit how much reaching and walking around you need to do before the loaf is shaped and you can wash them anew.

We generally shun meatloaf pans, which make infrequent appearances in these pages. There are two reasons: It's more difficult to slice meatloaf and cleanly remove those portions from a narrow pan in which the loaf is snugly ensconced, its sides wedged tight against the metal sides. Also, a meatloaf, as it cooks, often releases juices. If there's some space around the meatloaf, as there is if you cook it in a cast-iron skillet or in a rectangular baking pan of at least 9 by 13 inches, those juices have a place to pool and you can spoon them back over the loaf as it cooks or over the slices before you serve them. And if you're glazing the meatloaf, you can cover the top *and* brush the sides if it's in a vessel that allows you access to the sides. A tight loaf pan doesn't allow that access.

There are nonetheless situations in which we prefer and recommend a loaf pan—with certain vegetarian loaves, for example. Before cooking, they may not hold their shape well, and the loaf pan is a sort of mold that keeps the whole production together until it's had enough time in the oven to stiffen. So keep it in mind for loaves that in uncooked form are a bit looser, and for loaves whose ultimate appeal has much to do with their appearance. No matter how artful your eyes and nimble your hands, a loaf you've sculpted is never going to be as evenly, tidily proportioned as a loaf that a pan has sculpted for you.

A final note on pans: Beware one that's overly large, as the pooling juices are more likely to disperse, sizzle and evaporate during cooking.

If you've been turned off of meatloaf because you always find it dry, you haven't been eating the right meatloaf or the meatloaf you've been eating has been cooked too long, which is the distressing tendency of many meatloaf makers. Because they can't check—and go by—interior color as easily and reliably as when cooking, say, a chop, they err on the side of overcooking. They figure: It's only meatloaf. Well, disrespect your meatloaf and it will disrespect you.

We err in the opposite direction, if we err at all, and would encourage you to aim for medium-rare in meatloaves made of beef or lamb and for medium in meatloaves made of pork, chicken or turkey. For safety's sake, we provide the minimum temperature for these meats that's recommended by the FDA, and you can use a meat thermometer, which plunges easily into the center of a meatloaf. But some people pull their loaves out at a slightly lower temperature or go by sight, as most loaves do darken gradually as they cook, their glazes (if they have them) thickening. We've provided you with the cooking times that have worked for us and saved us from a dry meatloaf fate.

Cheese is your ally. If you're especially concerned about a moist meatloaf, choosing and making one that calls for a significant quantity of cheese, in particular a creamy cheese or one that melts quickly and thoroughly, is a smart strategy. In these pages you will find a range of cheeses that fit that bill: Cheddar, blue, feta. You will find pecorino, too, though that's less a moistener than it is a conveyor of sharp, salty punch. It's Parmesan's bossier sibling. Don't be afraid of it.

Don't be afraid of anything. Remember: Meatloaf is magnanimous, and it's supposed to be fun.

* * *

The fun of it has a lot to do with what a canny impersonator it is. Because it's a sponge for any number of ingredients, meatloaf can be made to taste shockingly like a dish that it in no way visually or aesthetically resembles. We have a meatloaf in these pages—it's the one with tortilla chips—that's a dead ringer, flavorwise, for a hard-shell taco. We have another that replicates the effect of hot Buffalo-style chicken wings dipped in blue cheese. And we have another that calls to mind not just a cheeseburger—which is to be expected, given the family relationship between meatloaf and hamburger—but a cheeseburger with fries.

Speaking of fries, we have meatloaves that incorporate a meat and a side that typically accompanies it (for example, mashed potatoes) into one creation that packs the punch of an entire dinner plate. That's also part of the fun and lure of meatloaf. An individual meatloaf sings in many octaves, like a choir, and has many personalities, like Sybil.

As we noted before, it doesn't have a place on most celebrated chefs' menus, but it definitely has a place in their hearts. We know this because we approached nearly a dozen of them to ask if they had a favorite meatloaf that they'd like to contribute to this book. Each and every one of them did, and a few even invented new recipes for this book. Michael Schwartz, a culinary god in Miami, did that with the kasha loaf in the chapter on meatless loaves. Mike Solomonov, a Philadelphia deity, did that with his lamb loaf. There's a whole nation of expert counsel in these pages, stretching from coast to coast.

These chefs' excitement was their acknowledgment that meatloaf commands more affection than actual respect and that it deserves some extra evangelism. You could be buried in the number of books devoted to cookies. You could climb to the top of the Pantheon in Rome on a winding staircase of books about pasta.

Meatloaf is a dish desperate for illumination. In the pages and recipes ahead, we give it precisely that, and what you'll see is a many-splendored thing. You'll also see a gift that keeps on giving. Unlike so many dishes that surrender their appeal when they lose their freshness, meatloaf often tastes better on Day Two and better still on Day Three. And meatloaf yields leftovers that work perfectly in, and as, a sandwich. Just tuck a slice of loaf between two slices of bread, add a few well-chosen accoutrements and voilà: lunch!

We've tagged the meatloaves in this book that, in our opinion, are the most sandwich-ready, the most sandwich-promising, and we've made suggestions for rolls, condiments and such. In almost every case you can leave the meatloaf cold. You can warm it up. It works either way. That's meatloaf—ever accommodating, ever flexible.

If, in the interest of generating leftovers, you want to upsize the recipes in this book—some of which serve only four people, others of which serve six to eight—you should feel free. Just bear in mind that the larger the loaf, the longer the cooking time, so adjust that time, adding 5 to 8 minutes for a loaf that's grown by 1.5 times and 8 to 15 minutes for a loaf that's doubled. You can also shrink any loaf in this book, lessening the cooking time. And, of course, adjust all of the ingredients accordingly. That's a simple matter of fractions, and if you're hopeless at math, well, we can't help you with that. But with meatloaf itself, we're at the ready. We're at your service. We're itching to take you on a tour through its possibilities.

Here we go.

Essential Equipment

~~~

One of the glories of meatloaf is that, by and large, it doesn't ask for any special equipment. Listed below are a few items that you truly must have, along with others that will make your loafing life a bit more effortless.

OVEN THERMOMETER

This is a good thing to have for all your cooking days. You may be surprised to learn that your oven runs hotter or cooler than the dial suggests. You can get this at the grocery store.

MEAT THERMOMETER

Yes, you can cut through the center of your loaves to see if they are done, but a thermometer does the work for you, gives you the assurances you need and prevents overcooking, which is your biggest risk with meatloaf.

We provide the USDA guidelines for internal temperatures. You should really follow them with pork. Lamb and ground beef have wiggle room if you prefer them medium-rare—and we mention that option when appropriate.

Nonstick loaf pan

Many of our loaves can be made in other pans, and in many cases we prefer it. But a loaf pan is needed for certain loaves, especially the vegetarian options, to help their structure. A nonstick pan is best because you will find that loaves slide more easily from it, and you will also enjoy having it around for making banana bread.

Rimmed baking sheet

You have one of these baking sheets around for making cookies. They are large enough to accommodate even the biggest loaves and the rims prevent grease or sauce from dripping onto the floor of your oven.

9-by-13-inch baking pan or dish

This is Frank's preferred meatloaf vessel, because it has room for sauce to pool around the sides of the loaf.

Basting brush

Optional, but easier to use than a spoon for glazing loaves. We prefer silicone versions.

Food processor

A few recipes call for it; it can be used to chop some veggies for loaves with lots of ingredients, too. Just make sure you know how to "pulse" and can do so with restraint. Excessive processing sometimes produces veggie paste in instances when it's not recommended. (When it is, we specify that in the recipe.)

BLENDER

Great for making some of the sauces accompanying some of the loaves.

PARCHMENT PAPER

We offer the options of aluminum foil or parchment paper. Frank loves the cleanup ease of the former, especially nonstick aluminum foil, which can work so well that you almost needn't clean the dish or pan afterward. Jennifer prefers the paper, which is usually used for baking, as it has better nonsticking properties than regular aluminum foil and can prevent over-browning on the bottom of the loaf.

CAST-IRON PAN

The absolute best for sautéing onions and other ingredients. Also, you can wipe it out and form your loaf in it and pop it right into the oven. This is Jennifer's favorite way to cook loaves.

SHARP KNIFE

Perhaps you are insulted by this suggestion, or perhaps you are a recent college graduate and have yet to purchase this item. Either way, you need one. Frank's favorite is a Wüsthof that Nora Ephron gave him as a thank-you for his blink-and-you-missed-him cameo in Julie & Julia, where he can be seen clapping idiotically at the arrival of a roasted duck.

A sharp knife not only helps to ensure that your loaf does not fall apart when it's sliced, but also makes chopping bearable and even fun: If you're struggling with this task, it's quite likely because your knife's a clunker or you've let it become dull. If you want to be extremely thorough and sophisticated about your loaf-ing—and about all your cooking—you might want to invest in a knife *sharpener* as well.

STANDING MIXER

There are a few recipes here that call for a mixer for combining the meat, because of the texture the mixer provides. You can substitute a hand mixer but it won't be quite the same. If you buy this, you will begin making a lot of cakes.

CANDY THERMOMETER

This is called for only in the recipe for the fried Brussels sprouts (page 240), but you really do need it if you're going to make that. These range in price greatly; buy the cheapest one and then immediately begin making caramels.

MUFFIN TINS, ESPECIALLY NONSTICK ONES

Yes, muffin tins. You're thinking: Have I strayed into the wrong book? What does an implement for breakfast food and cupcakes have to do with *meatloaf*? You will soon be educated. And you will see that muffin tins matter.

PORCELAIN OR GLASS RAMEKINS

Many meatloaf recipes call for the separate chopping of this and zesting of that and mincing of yet something else before the components get mixed together in a loaf, and a great way to store those components separately without running out of countertop or having too much to put into your dishwasher later is to use small ramekins in place of bowls. Sets of them are relatively easy to find and inexpensive to purchase.

ONE

Classics

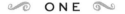

Frank: There's a place for veal in meatloaf, but it's limited. In the world at large, there's altogether too much veal in meatloaf. I think we're doing a great public service in not repeating that mistake.

Jenn: I think that's right. Let's get right out there and say it: Veal is sort of the truffle oil of meats. We think it adds flavor and elegance. But in reality, what the meatloaf world needs now is fat and more fat. (Also, salt.)

Frank: You've hit on the two central lessons of meatloaf cookery, our two greatest gifts to home cooks around the world. Number one, meatloaf is not diet food: Fat is flavor, and if you're using lean meats and never adding dairy, well, you're on your own. Godspeed to you. Two, a meatloaf is a sponge for salt. It laps up salt. It loves salt. It blossoms with salt.

Jenn: There is a lot of science behind why ground beef needs more salt than other forms, but we'll save that for later. Instead, let us pivot to other seasonings. The first time we pondered a tablespoon of *anything*, we shuddered a bit. But we soon realized that with rare exceptions, ground meat, particularly beef, takes a shine to all forms of herbs, spices, sauces and seasoning in generous quantities.

Frank: What was that Coco Chanel edict about accessories: Before you walk out the door, take two or three off? With meatloaf and seasonings it's the opposite: Add a few more. There's always room.

Jenn: Yes, in fact, as we tested our loaves, the biggest challenge was to fight the bland. Perhaps this is your own personal memory of meatloaf: someone's mother's overcooked, under-seasoned, sort of needlessly, unpleasantly crunchy slab of meat, swimming sadly under a small pond of ketchup. Not that we hate ketchup. In fact, we embrace it. We date it. We want to marry it. But we also want it to see other people.

Frank: Motherwise, I was blessed, not least because her meatloaf, an adaptation of which appears in this chapter (page 29), wasn't bland, or dry, at all. It also underscores some of what we've been discussing

here: Fatty cuts of ground
beef are what you want,
and you want plenty of
moisture and oomph.
Hers is a wet, tangy, sweet
loaf. Did your mom have a
meatloaf?

Jenn: No, my mom had a roast
beef. Salt only, served with
iceberg lettuce and bell
peppers and eaten in front of
Mary Tyler Moore. But I digress. Because the truth is that while most
meatloaves follow a fairly standard ingredient list and method—
ground beef, some seasoning, some binder and some glaze squished
together and baked—many families have added their own line to
the story over the years. Sometimes it reflects their ethnic heritage—
Italian ham, Middle Eastern spices—other times a single must-have
ingredient that distinguishes their loaf.

Frank: We have a terrific example of a family loaf in this chapter, from
the celebrated chef and TV personality Alex Guarnaschelli (page 45).
In fact we have family loaves scattered throughout the chapters that
follow. Toward the end of the book we'll share one from the long-
serving Republican senator from Maine, Susan Collins (page 213).
Not to pat ourselves on the back too often, though it sure does feel
good, but I think that in teasing something other than legislation
from the halls of Congress—something edible, no less—we have
done America proud.

Jenn: We don't mean to turn the meatloaf into another elegiac journey through the family kitchen. Meatloaf is not a meal you need to learn at anyone's elbow; it is as intuitive as playing with snow. Meatloaf memories in many cases stem from family frugality, a way to stretch a protein to feed a large family. Meatloaf is a place less to relive memories, although that is part of it, and perhaps more to make your own mark. If your mom used bell peppers, maybe you'd rather involve jalapeños. If your memories of meatloaf revolve around its uniformity, maybe you want to shake things up with some hard-boiled eggs. Our Eggs in Your Meatloaf recipe in this chapter (page 40) does precisely that. The point here is, even with classic meatloaves, find your voice!

Frank: We shouldn't forget pork. While ground beef is the logical, rightful building block for many a meatloaf, ground pork is right behind it, and it packs the flavor and fattiness that veal, to circle back to the beginning, often lacks. It's here in this chapter, in Painter's Meatloaf (page 37) and in Annie Miler's Home-Style Loaf with Cheddar and Parsley (page 32), and our recommendation for Clean Out the Fridge Meatloaf (page 50) is a combination of beef and pork.

Jenn: I would like to say something very important here, something that is going to change readers' lives in a manner of significance somewhere between meeting the right man and finding the proper moisturizer: Once you have formed your meatloaf batter, it is very helpful to pull off a tiny bit, make it into a small patty, fry it up in a pan and taste it. This will help you know whether your meat is going to bind, and if it needs a little more of this or that. Also, if you drink while you cook, as we do, it's nice to have a little snack. Chefs do this. So should everyone else.

Frank: Drinking while cooking? Well I *never*! Except sometimes for a glass of Chardonnay. Or a glass of Pinot Noir. Or a glass and a half. In reality I have a rule about *hard alcohol* while cooking, because a martini was once involved in a lasagna apocalypse that almost prompted the Italian government to formally rescind my ethnic heritage. But I do think the right measure of wine emboldens the cook, soothes the cook and brings the most important seasoning of all into the meatloaf process: joy. A meatloaf made with joy is a meatloaf eaten with abandon. Sew that onto a pillow.

Leslie Bruni's Sweet, Nostalgic Loaf

Serves 4

Most of us grew up with just one meatloaf, which is to say that most of us grew up deprived. If this was before 1975, that meatloaf was most likely mom's, and it probably got the bulk of its flavor from onions, ketchup and Worcestershire, the building blocks of meatloaf at its most basic and most kitschy.

They were and remain the building blocks of Leslie Bruni's meatloaf, too.

But Frank's mom had a few surprises up her sleeve: some brown sugar, which gives this meatloaf a restrained, gentle sweetness that's irresistible, and significant measures of tomato sauce, which help to keep it extra moist. We've in fact moistened it further by sautéing the onions, which Frank's mom left raw, and by replacing some of the bread crumbs with soaked white bread.

It's a populist meatloaf. It's a kid-friendly meatloaf, especially with the tang of raw onions tamed by the cooking of the onions. And this meatloaf is easily upsized by 1.5 times or 2 times. In the first case, keep it in the oven 5 to 7 minutes longer; in the second case, 10 to 12 minutes more, and in a significantly larger pan.

For us, it's pure nostalgia. For you, too, we bet.

1–2 tablespoons salted butter

1 medium-sized white or yellow onion, finely chopped

½ cup whole milk or half-and-half

3 slices white bread, not too thick, crusts removed

1½ pounds ground chuck or other high-fat ground beef

½ cup unseasoned bread crumbs

2 eggs, lightly beaten

2 8-ounce cans Hunt's tomato sauce or a similar canned, unseasoned tomato sauce

3 teaspoons Worcestershire sauce

2 tablespoons Dijon or other slightly zingy mustard

3 tablespoons white vinegar

3 tablespoons brown sugar (either dark or light is fine)

Salt and freshly ground black pepper to taste

1. Preheat the oven to 350 degrees F. Line a glass, metal or other kind of 13-by-9-inch baking pan with nonstick aluminum foil.

2. In a small or medium-sized skillet over low heat, melt only enough butter to coat the skillet. Add the onions and turn the heat to medium, stirring the onions occasionally and cooking until they soften and turn slightly translucent, no more than 12 minutes.

3. Meanwhile, pour the milk or half-and-half into a shallow bowl, place each side of each slice of bread in the liquid just long enough to moisten it and then transfer the bread slices to a large mixing bowl. Discard the leftover milk or half-and-half.

4. Add the beef, bread crumbs, eggs and half of one of the cans of tomato sauce to the bread in the large mixing bowl, and blend together with

your clean hands, using a kneading motion, just until the ingredients are fully incorporated. Transfer the mixture to the baking pan, shaping it into a loaf whose width is consistent except at the slightly tapered ends.

5. Separately, in a medium-sized bowl, whisk the remaining 1½ cans of tomato sauce with the Worcestershire, mustard, vinegar, brown sugar, salt and pepper until the sugar has dissolved. Pour the sauce over the loaf so that it coats the top and pools at the sides.

6. Cook for 1 hour to 1 hour 15 minutes, depending on the desired doneness; 145 degrees F is perfect for medium-rare, which we think is best. Remove the pan from the oven and let the loaf rest, uncovered, for 10 minutes. Then slice it into individual servings and use a large spoon to ladle sauce from the pan over each portion.

Leslie Bruni's Sweet Nostalgic Loaf has a dance of sweet and vinegary flavors that vaguely recall North Carolina barbecue. So treat the leftovers the way you would pulled pork and make the same kind of sandwich with them: Heat a slice briefly in the oven or leave it cold; then dress it with a heap of mayonnaise-based coleslaw, which provides your condiment and your vegetal crunch in one fell swoop (or scoop, as the case may be). Your cradle is a fluffy, sturdy hamburger bun or potato roll. Your satisfaction is guaranteed.

Annie Miler's Home-Style Loaf with Cheddar and Parsley

Serves 6 to 9

We used to meet our friend Nora Ephron for lunch at Clementine, Annie Miler's restaurant in the Century City area of Los Angeles, because all three of us loved Miler's dedication to hearty American classics: tuna melts, Sloppy Joes. And as soon as we set out to do this book, we knew that we wanted a meatloaf recipe from her.

Annie came through with one in perfect keeping with her unpretentious approach. It's a no-fuss counterpoint to the fanciful meatloaves in the pages ahead, and it's a testament to the effectiveness of fail-safe components in prudent proportion.

Miler sizes this for a big family (or for leftovers), giving you the measurements for a pair of loaves. But you can absolutely halve the recipe and do a loaf that's solitary, uncoupled, like Bridget Jones before Mark Darcy came along. She means for you to relax and customize—hence the wiggle room in the recipe—and told us: "I generally try to avoid being super-specific, especially for something as homey as meatloaf."

Feel free to up the amount of cheese a bit; the recipe works well that way. Know that these loaves are smaller than the ones you might be used to, because the bread factor is minimal. And to ensure tenderness, subtract 5 to 10 minutes from the cooking time if you're doing just one loaf.

> 1 extra-thick slice hearty country white bread, or 3 slices thin white
>   bread (crusts left on)
>
> 2/3 cup whole milk
>
> 1 large egg, lightly beaten
>
> 2 pounds ground beef of your choice (we recommend chuck)
>
> 1 pound ground pork
>
> 3/4 cup finely diced yellow, white or Spanish onion
>
> 3/4 cup diced Cheddar cheese, yellow or orange, not too sharp
>
> 2 teaspoons Worcestershire sauce
>
> 6 tablespoons ketchup, plus more for coating
>
> 1 tablespoon yellow mustard
>
> 1 tablespoon kosher salt
>
> 1/4 teaspoon freshly ground
>   black pepper
>
> 2 tablespoons
>   chopped fresh
>   flat-leaf parsley

1. Preheat the oven to 350 degrees F and line a large rimmed baking sheet with parchment paper or aluminum foil.

2. In a small bowl, soak the bread slice or slices in the milk for several minutes. Then tear the bread into pieces, add the egg and stir the mixture together to further break up the bread and to achieve an oatmeal-like consistency.

3. In a large bowl, use your clean hands to gently combine the bread-milk-egg mixture with the rest of the ingredients.

4. Divide the mixture in half, shape the halves into identically sized footballs and place them on the prepared baking sheet. Generously coat the top and sides of each loaf with ketchup.

5. Bake for 50 to 60 minutes, depending on the desired doneness, or until the internal temperature reaches 155 to 160 degrees F.

6. Remove the baking sheet from the oven and let the loaves rest, uncovered, for about 10 minutes, and then slice and serve.

Beef, Pork and Cremini Mushroom Loaf

Serves 6

hile chopping and dicing are the main activities of meatloaf making, the food processor can be a handy alternative to the chef's knife. When you use the food processor, you're essentially turning your veggies into paste and giving them a texture similar to the meat. The incorporation of everything is seamless.

We skip any sautéing here, which gives this recipe the advantage of being faster than any chop-chop-chop version—unless you, like us, have to lug your food processor from a cabinet in the next room, where it may or may not be buried under a juicer, a large platter and some sort of ceramic tea set purchased on a honeymoon with a man to whom you are no longer married.

3 slices white sandwich bread

⅓ cup whole milk

1 large carrot, peeled and
    roughly chopped

1 cup cremini mushrooms,
    wiped clean and stemmed

1 small onion, quartered

2 cloves garlic, cut in half

1½ pounds ground beef chuck

½ pound ground pork

1 large egg

½ cup ketchup

2 teaspoons kosher salt

Freshly ground black pepper
    to taste

1. Preheat the oven to 350 degrees F. Line a baking sheet with aluminum foil.

2. Place the bread in a food processor and pulse until fine. Transfer the bread to a small bowl, add the milk and set it aside for about 10 minutes, until the milk has been absorbed.

3. Put the carrot, mushrooms, onion and garlic in the food processor and pulse until fully ground into something resembling paste.

4. In a large bowl, combine the beef, pork, egg, ¼ cup of the ketchup, and the salt and pepper. Add the bread and the vegetables and mix gently with your clean hands only until all the ingredients are integrated.

5. Place the meat mixture on the prepared baking sheet, and form it into an even rectangular loaf.

chemini

6. Bake, brushing the top twice with the remaining ¼ cup ketchup, for 45 to 55 minutes or until the internal temperature reaches 160 degrees F. Remove the baking sheet from the oven and let the meatloaf rest, uncovered, for 10 minutes before slicing and serving.

Painter's Meatloaf

Serves 4

If you want a meatloaf that looks as good as it tastes, this is your loaf, speckled with color. That's why we've given it its name.

It's an adaptation of a meatloaf frequently made by Lisa Kelly, an acquaintance of ours on Manhattan's Upper West Side. It placed second to the Greek Loaf with Lamb and Feta at a dinner party that doubled as a meatloaf cook-off, with each guest bringing a beloved meatloaf and all of the guests gorging on the others'. That's where we fell for it—and where we learned that even small combinations of the right spices, in this case nutmeg and cumin, really make a loaf distinctive. That's where we vowed to harangue Lisa until she gave us the recipe. No haranguing was necessary. She's a lovely woman. With a lovely meatloaf.

1 tablespoon vegetable oil

1 small onion, diced (about ¾ cup)

1 carrot, peeled and finely chopped

¼ cup finely chopped green bell pepper

½ cup finely chopped red bell pepper

1 cup torn pieces of white bread (crusts removed)

½ cup half-and-half or whole milk

½ pound ground beef chuck

½ pound ground pork

2 eggs, lightly beaten

⅔ cup ketchup

2 teaspoons kosher salt

½ teaspoon ground cumin

¼ teaspoon grated nutmeg

¼ teaspoon cayenne pepper, or ½ teaspoon Sriracha

A few grinds of fresh black pepper

1. Preheat the oven to 325 degrees F.

2. Heat the oil in a medium-sized skillet over medium heat. Add the onions and sauté until soft, anywhere from 7 to 10 minutes.

3. Add the chopped carrots and bell peppers and sauté until tender, about 8 minutes. Remove the skillet from the heat and let the vegetables cool.

4. In a small bowl, briefly soak the bread pieces in the half-and-half or milk, and then squeeze them to remove the excess liquid. (Discard the liquid.)

5. In a large bowl, use your clean hands to mix together the soaked bread, meats, eggs, ⅓ cup of the ketchup, and the salt, cumin, nutmeg, cayenne or Sriracha, and pepper until well combined. Then fold in the vegetable mixture until thoroughly mixed.

6. Pat the mixture into a 5-by-9-inch loaf pan, and coat the top of the loaf with the remaining ⅓ cup ketchup.

7. Bake the loaf for 1 hour and then check it; bake for another few minutes if the loaf seems to need it or if the internal temperature hasn't yet reached 160 degrees F. Remove the pan from the oven and let the loaf rest, uncovered, for 10 minutes.

8. Slice and serve.

Eggs in Your Meatloaf

Serves 6

Several nations—notably Greece, Germany and Hungary—have versions of meatloaf featuring boiled eggs in the middle. On the surface, this might seem like protein overload, or Easter in your Christmas. But there's aesthetic pleasure in cutting into a loaf and seeing the lovely white and yellow in the middle, and then there's the bonus of a custardy texture and flavor.

We thought this would be delicious topped with a sweet glaze, but we had to cut back on that because the loaf itself is a tiny bit sweet, possibly because of the carrot. So we reduced the brown sugar and upped the heat for the glaze, hitting the perfect pitch. Sage adds an unexpected earthy twist. And this dish is pretty on the table.

LOAF

2 tablespoons extra-virgin olive oil

1 carrot, peeled and finely chopped

1 small stalk celery, finely chopped

1 small yellow onion, finely chopped

2 tablespoons minced fresh sage

2 cups roughly chopped bread, preferably sourdough and
preferably stale

½ cup whole milk

1 pound ground beef

1 pound ground veal

2 cloves garlic, minced

½ cup grated Parmigiano-Reggiano cheese

1 tablespoon Worcestershire sauce

1 tablespoon Dijon mustard

1 tablespoon kosher salt

Freshly ground black pepper to taste

1 raw, large egg, lightly beaten

4 hard-boiled eggs, peeled

2 slices nitrate-free bacon

GLAZE

2 tablespoons brown sugar

¼ cup ketchup

2 tablespoons hot sauce

1. Preheat the oven to 350 degrees F. Line a large baking sheet with aluminum foil.

2. In a medium-sized frying pan, warm the olive oil over medium heat. Add the carrots, celery, onions and sage and cook, stirring often, until the vegetables begin to soften, 8 to 10 minutes. Remove the pan from the heat and let the mixture cool for 10 minutes.

3. In a small bowl, combine the bread and milk. Let it sit for 5 minutes, and then squeeze out the excess milk and place the bread in a large bowl. Add the ground beef, veal, garlic, cheese, Worcestershire, Dijon and sautéed vegetables. Mix thoroughly with your clean hands. Season with the salt and a generous grinding of pepper. Add the beaten egg and mix everything together thoroughly.

4. Put the meatloaf mixture on the baking sheet, and using a spatula or your hands, pat it into a loaf that is 9 to 10 inches long and 4 to 5 inches wide. Make a depression down the center of the rectangle, and arrange the hard-boiled eggs lengthwise in it. Then, with your hands, pat the mixture over the eggs to form an oval-shaped loaf. Make sure

the eggs are completely covered by the meat mixture. Top the meatloaf with the slices of bacon.

5. To make the glaze, combine the brown sugar, ketchup and hot sauce in a small saucepan over low heat and cook until the brown sugar is melted. Mix well, and brush the glaze over the top of the loaf.

6. Bake until the meatloaf is cooked through and thoroughly browned on top, about 50 minutes, or until the internal temperature reaches 160 degrees F. Remove the baking sheet from the oven and let the loaf rest, uncovered, for 5 to 10 minutes.

7. Cut the loaf into thick slices and arrange them on a platter. Spoon the pan juices over them and serve.

When turning leftover meatloaf into a sandwich, tease out the themes already present. **Eggs in Your Meatloaf** brings to mind breakfast (the eggs) and Italy (the Parmesan). Build on that. Heat a teaspoon of olive oil in a skillet and then, turning the heat up, quickly sear a slice of the loaf on both sides, as you would a slab of bacon. Tuck it between toasted halves of an English muffin along with some sliced tomato and a sprinkling of chopped fresh herbs—preferably basil and parsley—or a tangle of fresh arugula. Optional: Grate Parmesan over the inside of the sandwich to echo the cheese in the loaf.

Alex Guarnaschelli's Mom's Meatloaf

Serves 6 to 8

The celebrity chef Alex Guarnaschelli learned her trade at the elbow of her cookbook-editing mom, Maria Guarnaschelli. While Alex is the master of many forms of fine dining, she still adores her mother's take on meatloaf.

Alex's desire for meatloaf in general was seeded, she told us, by an old Irish bar near the Manhattan apartment where she grew up. The aromas of beer and of cabbage that had been cooking for hours would waft into the street, and she could look inside and see the cooks slicing giant wedges of meatloaf that she longed to try.

"My mother's tiny loaf paled in comparison the first time I saw her pull it from the oven," Alex remembered—but then she tasted the grassiness of its tarragon, the tang of its sour cream, the flavors of multiple meats combined.

"If you have time," Alex added, "grind your own beef, using brisket and chuck cuts, and your own pork, using shoulder cuts."

1 pound ground beef

3/4 pound ground pork or dark turkey meat

1 teaspoon paprika

1 tablespoon kosher salt

1 teaspoon freshly ground black pepper

1 cup panko bread crumbs

2/3 cup ketchup, plus extra for brushing

1 cup sour cream

10–12 sprigs fresh curly parsley,
   stemmed and chopped

8–10 sprigs fresh tarragon,
   stemmed and chopped

3 large eggs, lightly beaten

1 teaspoon vegetable or
   canola oil

1 medium yellow onion,
   minced (roughly 1
   cup)

2 cloves garlic, minced

1. Preheat the oven to 400 degrees F. Line a rimmed baking sheet (the rim helps the loaf to form a crust) with parchment paper.

2. Put the beef and the pork or turkey in a large bowl and gently knead them together with your clean hands. Add the paprika, salt, pepper, bread crumbs, ketchup, sour cream, parsley, tarragon and eggs. Mix to blend.

3. Heat a small saucepan over medium heat and add the vegetable oil. When the oil begins to smoke, lower the heat and add a small piece of the meatloaf mixture. Cook for 1 to 2 minutes on each side. Remove the sample from the pan and taste it. Check the seasoning. If the cooked sample is too moist, add more bread crumbs to the mixture in the bowl. If too dry, add an extra egg.

4. Add the onions and garlic to the same saucepan and cook over medium heat, stirring from time to time, until they become translucent, 3 to 5 minutes. Add the onions and garlic to the meat mixture and mix to blend.

5. Mold the mixture into a loaf shape on your lined baking sheet and bake, undisturbed, for 15 minutes. Then brush it with additional ketchup and lower the oven temperature to 350 degrees F.

6. Continue to bake until the loaf is firm to the touch or it has an internal temperature of 150 degrees F, about 45 minutes. Remove the baking sheet from the oven, pour off any excess grease and allow the loaf to rest, uncovered, for 10 to 15 minutes before serving. Brush again with ketchup, if desired.

Joan Futter's Meatloaf

Meatloaf means memories, and for our editor, Deb Futter, this is particularly poignant. Her mother, Joan, no longer cooks, and Deb had to re-create her childhood favorite—made in Joan's kitchen every week and then served as leftovers for days—from her own recollections. Was the recipe off the back of a cracker or cornflakes box or a package of Lipton soup mix? Maybe. Perhaps it was from a women's magazine? She can't remember. Either way, it's a classic—some crumbs as the binder and ground beef seasoned with soup mix. Deb takes a bite of this version, reconstructed in her own family's kitchen decades later, and connects to her mother, voice and all, each time.

1 tablespoon olive oil

1 large onion, chopped

2½ pounds ground beef round

1 tablespoon dried basil

2 eggs, lightly beaten

2 cups Kellogg's Corn Flake Crumbs (or other brand)

½ cup whole milk

½ cup ketchup

1 package Lipton Recipe Secrets onion soup mix

1. Preheat the oven to 350 degrees F.

2. Warm the olive oil in a large skillet over medium heat and sauté the onions until soft and fragrant, about 15 minutes.

3. While the onions cook, combine the rest of the ingredients in a large bowl, and mix together with your clean hands.

4. Add the sautéed onions to the mixture, mix well and transfer it to a round glass or ceramic baking dish.

5. Bake for 1 hour to 1 hour 15 minutes, depending on the desired doneness; 145 degrees F is perfect for medium-rare. Remove the dish from the oven and let the meatloaf rest, uncovered, for 10 minutes before slicing and serving

Clean Out the Fridge Meatloaf

Serves 4

*S*ometimes, at the end of the week, we find ourselves with some ground meat that we have failed to cook. We then scramble to make it into something before it spoils. There is often a little of this and a little of that hanging around as well. This recipe pulls together your random meat and that-which-could-have-become-compost into a nice dinner.

If you don't have a carrot, no worries. If you would rather throw in some other vegetables, go ahead and toss them in instead. Hate smoked paprika? How about some cayenne pepper? Shallots can stand in for the onion. It's all very wartime, with a modern twist: Wear a fetching period headscarf while you cook, and perhaps lecture your children about economizing while they download expensive apps.

2 teaspoons neutral oil, such as vegetable oil

1 small yellow onion, chopped

2 teaspoons salt, plus a pinch

1 large carrot, peeled and diced

2 cloves garlic, chopped

½ pound mushrooms, preferably cremini but any will do, roughly chopped (about 1 cup)

1½ pounds ground meat: the best choice is a mix of beef and pork

1 heaping tablespoon smoked paprika

1 large egg, lightly beaten

½ cup unseasoned bread crumbs (panko is best), plus ¼ cup if needed

½ cup ketchup

1. Preheat the oven to 325 degrees F, and line a large rimmed baking sheet with aluminum foil.

2. Warm the oil in a medium-sized skillet over low to medium heat. Add the onions and a generous pinch of salt, and sauté until they are soft and fragrant, about 10 minutes. Reduce the heat and add the carrots; cook for another 5 minutes; then add the garlic and cook for 2 more minutes. Add the mushrooms and cook until they have given off all their liquid and become soft and fragrant, about 5 minutes.

3. Put the skillet ingredients in a large bowl, and add the meat, paprika, 2 teaspoons salt, the egg and the ½ cup bread crumbs; mix well with your clean hands. If the mixture does not hold together well—this may depend on the meat used—add the extra ¼ cup bread crumbs. Form a loaf on the prepared baking sheet. Brush the loaf with the ketchup.

4. Bake for 50 minutes, and then check for doneness; the internal temperature should be 160 degrees F. If it isn't, bake for another 10 minutes or so. Remove the baking sheet from the oven and let the loaf rest, uncovered, for 10 minutes; then slice and serve.

TWO

Around the World

Jenn: I would like to inform you that South Africa has a national meatloaf, even though it isn't exactly a loaf. It's a casserole of sorts. It involves curry. It involves apples. It involves something that you really love and that's uniquely suited to meatloaf—La Lamb. But what makes this loaf, which is apparently one of the most beloved dishes of South Africa, *really* unique is a surprise custard top, which sits upon the meat like an elegant top hat. Our South African Bobotie Loaf (page 81) captures all of that.

Frank: I have a few strong reactions, presented here in no particular order. First, I am so glad you gave lamb that courtesy title—La Lamb—and we may thus, fittingly, speak of it as we do La Deneuve or La Streep. Second, I am distraught. A decade ago, I visited South Africa but at the time knew nothing of its meatloaf. So while I scarfed down more jumbo prawns than I thought the oceans of this gluttonous world could hold, I was loaf-deprived.

Jenn: This chapter is where things get more exciting. Those of us in the United States think of meatloaf as a classic American dish, and as

53

you and I explained to readers in the introduction to this book, it is indeed that. But other nations have their own versions of a meatloaf, even if they don't precisely call it that. What's more, American meatloaves, reflecting our general national ethos, take well to the spices and flavors of the rest of the world. I am particularly interested in the Korean-influenced meatloaf brought to us by the great Bobby Flay (page 61), which I find both a fun twist on the Korean taco movement that has engulfed us over the last few years and an extension of the special relationship that has long existed—*katchi kapshida*—between the United States and South Korea.

Frank: Bobby was a champ to give us this loaf, because he and I have a fraught history. Back when I was the *Times* restaurant critic, I downgraded his seminal restaurant, Mesa Grill, from two stars to one, and while he left a voicemail for me the next day thanking me at least for the compliment of my close attention, he later said in an interview with another journalist that it was one of his saddest moments as a chef. But we became e-mail buddies years later, after I left the job, and I've been a fan of his subsequent restaurants and fully recognize his talent, which he lavishes on a loaf in this chapter.

Jenn: So in other words, meatloaf heals the world? Sticking with Asia, let's talk Chinese food. Like so many Americans, I deeply adore its intense flavors, from five-spice powder to sesame oil. And I longed to invent a loaf that I could eat at Christmas—Jewish Christmas, that is. You no doubt know that when your people head to church or encircle a pine tree every December 25, my people hit Sichuan Kitchen. The loaf here (page 65) is for Jews on Christmas—or for everyone anytime—and it reflects some of the best seasonings of Chinese-style beef.

Frank: This chapter, I realize, isn't just about the wide world of meatloaf. It's about the DNA of one Jennifer Steinhauer and one Frank Bruni. To wit: the Pork and Beef Polpettone with Pancetta (page 57) is a meaty, loaf-y ode to Italy, home of my ancestors and even my own home from 2002 to 2004, when I was stationed in Rome for the *Times*. What I love about this loaf is how faithfully it evokes some of the flavors and flourishes I associate most strongly with Italian cooking. Also, it has pecorino. Pecorino, which appears with some frequency in these pages, is a meatloaf power player, contributing the tenderizing qualities of dairy and the punch of salt. Pecorino: yet another pearl of wisdom from you and me, Jenn, to the world.

Jenn: Is IKEA another country? I sort of think so. But let's stick with its actual roots, Sweden, another great meatloaf capital. We use the classic meat mix employed by our favorite place to buy beds that are impossible to put together and require some sort of center board that makes you go back to the store three times, which is fine because: *more meatballs*. And we offer you the recipe for the all-important gravy that puts the Swedish in those IKEA balls. While the classic topper for them would be a sauce of lingonberries, we suggest a dab of raspberry jam, which rounds out our Swedish Meatball Loaf (page 77) perfectly.

Frank: OK, let's move beyond berries. Let's go to France, where there are many berries—I feel the need to acknowledge this—but where neither the sturdiest culinary traditions nor our Auvergne-Style Loaf with Prunes (page 68) depends on them. Though we do bring some fruit into play. It's prune time!

Jenn: France, like so many countries, has foodways that are specific to a given city or region. It is thus with Avignon, which sits at the crossroads of Provence, Ventoux and the Camargue and which offers the world a loaf that's apparently consumed only there. Its key component is prunes, which we fleck throughout this loaf, and we add Cognac as a further nod to the region. It's a bit boozy, and reminiscent of pâté. Ready your passport.

Pork and Beef Polpettone with Pancetta

Serves 6 to 8

Time for a little Italian lesson. The Italian word for "meatball" is *polpetta*, though you will sometimes trip across the word *polpettina*. Those extra letters, in the form of the adorable suffix -ina, signal a *small* meatball. Swap that suffix for -one and you've flagged something *larger* than its usual self.

Polpettone essentially means "large meatball" and also happens to be the Italian word for meatloaf, thereby supporting our contention, back in the introduction of this book, that a meatloaf is in many ways a meatball with great ambition, even delusions of grandeur.

It's not just the name of this meatloaf that's Italian; it's the flavor, too. Be sure to use pancetta and not conventional American bacon, which isn't cut as thick and will cook into crumbly bits. Be sure to use a cheese that's sharper than Parmesan, as we've specified here. Stick to the Italian script and you wind up with something that tastes, well, like a gargantuan meatball.

There's *niente* wrong with that.

1 cup whole milk

2–3 slices thick white bread, crusts removed, roughly chopped

   (about 2 cups)

⅓ cup minced pancetta (often available packaged this way)

1 small onion, finely chopped (about ½ cup)

1 teaspoon olive oil (optional)

2 cloves garlic, minced

1 pound ground veal

1 pound ground pork

⅓ cup chopped fresh flat-leaf parsley

1 teaspoon grated lemon zest

2 heaping tablespoons tomato paste

1 teaspoon dried oregano

1 teaspoon dried basil

½ cup grated Pecorino Romano cheese (Locatelli brand is best)

1 large egg, lightly beaten

1 teaspoon kosher salt

¼ teaspoon freshly
    ground black pepper

1. Preheat the oven to 375 degrees F. Line a 9-by-13-inch (or larger) baking pan with aluminum foil.

2. Pour the milk into a medium bowl, add the bread and let it sit to absorb the milk, stirring once, about 10 minutes. Remove the bread from the milk, put it on paper towels and let the excess milk drip off. Then place the bread in a large bowl and set it aside. (Discard the milk.)

3. While the bread is draining, cook the pancetta in a large cast-iron skillet over medium heat until it is cooked through, about 8 minutes. Transfer it to a plate lined with paper towels, leaving the drippings in the skillet.

4. Put the onions in the same skillet, and add a teaspoon of olive oil if the drippings seem skimpy. Cook over low heat for about 10 minutes, until soft. Add the garlic and cook for another 2 to 4 minutes.

5. Transfer the onions and garlic to the bowl containing the bread. Add all the remaining ingredients and the pancetta. Mix thoroughly with your clean hands. Shape the mixture into a loaf in the prepared baking pan.

6. Bake for 45 minutes, and then check for doneness; the internal temperature should be close to 160 degrees F. If it isn't, bake for a few more minutes.

7. Remove the pan from the oven, cover it lightly with foil and let the meatloaf rest for at least 10 minutes. Slice and serve.

In many an Italian-American home, there's no more mouthwatering tradition than cooking, in a skillet slicked with olive oil, sausage, peppers (green, red or both) and onions, the caramelized amalgam of which is served as a hero or submarine. We suggest replacing the sausage with the **Pork and Beef Polpettone with Pancetta** or with the **Volpe Family Loaf with Ham** (page 190), slices of which should be seared quickly, after the peppers and onions are done, in the oil left behind. *Note:* The peppers and onions should be cut into thick slivers, not chopped, before they're cooked, and should be limp when done. If you have some fresh parsley, chop it and sprinkle it on the sandwich.

Bobby Flay's Korean-Style Meatloaf with Spicy Glaze

Serves 8

Demonstrating that chefs are not like us, Bobby Flay concocted and then prepared this exotic meatloaf on the spot during an episode of the Food Network's *Beat Bobby Flay*, a reality show in which other chefs go head-to-head against him. The flavors for this dish were inspired by *bibimbap*, a signature Korean rice dish that includes *gochujang*, the classic Korean chile bean paste. It's generally topped with a fried egg, then all mixed up at the end.

We won't lie, home cooks: This dish takes effort, including a run to your Asian market for the gochujang and kimchi. It also takes time. You're frying shallots in the beginning, you're frying eggs at the end. Either of these steps can be skipped if you want to reduce the time and calories involved. But know that the effort pays off: This is a dinner-party-worthy loaf, designed to impress your guests, who will no doubt ask you how you learned to make it.

Just tell them Bobby taught you.

FRIED SHALLOTS

1½ cups canola oil

½ cup rice flour

Salt and freshly ground black pepper to taste

3 large shallots, thinly sliced

LOAF

¼ cup gochujang

1 tablespoon clover honey

3 tablespoons low-sodium soy sauce

2 teaspoons canola oil

3 cloves garlic, finely chopped

2 tablespoons finely grated fresh ginger

¼ teaspoon Calabrian chile flakes

1 cup prepared kimchi, drained well and chopped

2 large eggs

2 tablespoons fish sauce

2 teaspoons toasted sesame oil

¾ pound ground beef chuck (80/20)

¾ pound ground pork (80/20)

¾ cup panko bread crumbs

FRIED EGG TOPPING

2 tablespoons unsalted butter

As many eggs as slices to be served

Kosher salt and freshly ground black pepper to taste

1. Preheat the oven to 375 degrees F. Line a rimmed baking sheet with parchment paper.

2. Cook the shallots: Pour the canola oil into a medium saucepan and heat it to 360 degrees F (use a deep-frying thermometer). In a bowl, whisk together the flour and ½ cup of water, and season with salt and pepper. Dredge the shallot slices in the batter, remove them with a slotted spoon and fry in the hot oil until they are crisp and golden brown. Drain the shallots on a plate lined with paper towels and season them with salt. Set aside.

3. Now get started on the loaf: In a small bowl, whisk together the gochujang, honey and 1 tablespoon of the soy sauce; set the glaze aside.

4. Heat the oil in a medium-sized sauté pan over medium heat. Add the garlic, ginger and chile flakes and cook for 45 seconds. Add the kimchi

and toss to combine. Transfer the mixture to a plate and let it cool for 10 minutes.

5. In a large bowl, whisk together the eggs, the remaining 2 tablespoons of soy sauce, the fish sauce and the sesame oil. Add the kimchi mixture and mix to combine. Add the beef, pork and bread crumbs, and mix gently to combine. Put the mixture on the prepared baking sheet and form it into a loaf about 12 inches long, 6 inches wide and 2 inches thick. Brush the top with the gochujang glaze, and bake in the oven until the loaf is golden brown and the internal temperature registers 155 degrees F, about 1 hour. Remove the baking sheet from the oven, loosely tent the loaf with foil and let it rest for 10 minutes.

6. While the meatloaf rests, make the topping: Melt the butter in a medium-sized nonstick sauté pan over medium heat. Crack 2 eggs at a time into the pan, season with salt and pepper and cook until the white is set and the yellow is partially set. Gently flip them over and cook for 30 seconds on the other side.

7. Slice the loaf, place a fried egg on each slice, top with the fried shallots and serve.

Jewish Christmas Loaf

We invented this loaf—named for the urban tradition of Jewish families trekking to Chinese restaurants on Christmas—to reflect some of our most treasured Chinese seasonings and flavors. We've tucked five-spice powder, soy sauce and sesame oil into a rich slab of ground beef. Then, for a climactic punch of heat and flavor, we turn to Asian garlic sauce (widely available in Asian grocery stores and at specialty markets like Whole Foods), which contains not just garlic but coarsely ground chiles as well.

This recipe uses a tad more uncooked oats—the innocuously flavored workhorse of binders—than many other loaves call for, because this particular meat mixture would otherwise be too wet. And over several tests of this recipe, we doubled the glaze from our first try because guests wanted more, more, more. It mingles with the pan juices and should be scooped up and spooned over the slices of loaf for anyone who wants that, which should be everyone.

LOAF

2 teaspoons toasted sesame oil

2 large shallots, finely chopped

2 pounds ground beef

1⅓ cups quick-cooking oats

2 eggs, lightly whisked

1 stalk celery, finely chopped

2 teaspoons five-spice powder

1 tablespoon soy sauce

1 tablespoon sesame seeds

½ cup finely chopped fresh cilantro

½ cup spicy Asian garlic sauce

GLAZE

2 tablespoons soy sauce

2 tablespoons spicy Asian garlic sauce

6 tablespoons ketchup

1. Preheat the oven to 350 degrees F. Line a rimmed baking sheet or a 9-by-13-inch baking dish with aluminum foil or parchment paper.

2. Warm the sesame oil in a medium-sized skillet over low heat. Add the shallots and sauté until they are soft, about 10 minutes. Let the shallots cool a bit.

3. In a large bowl, combine all the remaining loaf ingredients with the shallots and their oil. Mix thoroughly with your clean hands.

4. Pull off some of the meatloaf batter and create a tiny slider-sized burger; cook it in the still-slick skillet for a few minutes, until cooked through. Taste, and adjust the seasonings in accordance with your preferences.

5. On the prepared baking sheet or baking dish, form the mixture into a loaf with a uniform width from end to end.

6. To make the glaze, stir the soy sauce, garlic sauce and ketchup together in a small bowl. Slather the glaze over the top of the loaf, letting some drip off the sides.

7. Bake for about 1 hour 10 minutes or until the internal temperature reaches 155 degrees F. Remove the baking sheet from the oven and let the meatloaf rest, uncovered, for 10 minutes before slicing and serving. Spoon any sauce that has gathered around the loaf generously over the slices.

Auvergne-Style Loaf with Prunes

Serves 6

One of the most delightful aspects of traveling, especially in Europe, is the discovery of regional specialties, mainstays in their town or area that cannot be found even twenty miles away. So it is with this loaf, often referred to as pounti and peculiar to the largely rural region of Auvergne in central France.

Essentially a pork terrine, pounti is always dotted with prunes and is made rich through the addition of milk or cream. We nod to that tradition with a loaf that's plenty porky, but we also incorporate our own cheeky twists, which pay homage to pâté, such as Cognac and the warm flavors of nutmeg and cloves. The result is a hearty and earthy loaf that's perfect on a cold, raw day.

You may be startled by the presence of potato, which is our binder of choice for this recipe. You may fear that it will make the mixture too wet. It won't, and using your hands is key to integrating it into everything else. Don't use your thickest bacon here—it will increase the cooking time.

And save the leftovers. This loaf tastes great—some would argue best—after being reheated on Day Two.

1 medium russet potato, peeled and cut into 8 pieces

¼ cup whole milk

¼ cup Cognac

4 slices bacon

1 small onion, diced

1 clove garlic, minced

1½ pounds ground pork

½ pound ground veal

1 large egg, lightly beaten

10 prunes, pitted and roughly
   chopped

1 tablespoon kosher salt

½ teaspoon freshly ground black pepper

½ teaspoon grated nutmeg

½ teaspoon ground cloves

½ teaspoon ground ginger

1 cup finely chopped flat-leaf parsley leaves

1. Preheat the oven to 350 degrees F.

2. Fill a medium-sized saucepan with water and bring it to a boil. Add the potato pieces and cook until soft, about 15 minutes. Transfer them to a small bowl, add the milk and Cognac and mash thoroughly. Set aside.

3. In a medium-sized frying pan set over medium heat, cook 2 slices of the bacon until crisp. Set them aside until cool, and then crumble into fairly small bits.

4. Remove the excess fat from the pan, and return it to low heat. Add the

onions and cook until they are soft, about 7 minutes. Add the garlic and cook for another 2 minutes until all is soft and fragrant.

5. In a large bowl, use your clean hands to combine the meats (including the crumbled becon), egg, prunes, salt and pepper, spices and parsley, massaging it all together. Then add the cooked onions and the mashed potatoes, mixing with your hands only to the point where everything is incorporated.

6. In a large cast-iron pan, form the mixture into a loaf and drape it with the remaining 2 slices of bacon. Bake until the internal temperature reaches 160 degrees F and the bacon on the top is cooked through, about 1 hour 20 minutes. Let rest ten minutes, uncovered, before slicing and serving.

tomorrow's LUNCH

When in France, stick to a French approach. That means cutting a thin slice or slices of the **Auvergne-Style Loaf with Prunes** and tucking the meat into a baguette, toasted or untoasted. The meat can be cold or reheated, in accordance with your convenience and desires; if you're toasting the baguette, consider using cold meat for the contrast. Spread some Dijon mustard on the meat to balance the sweetness of the prunes, and for a final Gallic flourish, dice some cornichons—those tiny pickled gherkins you see on charcuterie plates—and sprinkle them atop the mustard.

Cheesy Chorizo Loaf

Serves 6

One of the surest, easiest shortcuts to a meatloaf with a lively mix of seasonings and optimal tenderness is the use of a sausage that packs its own spiciness and fattiness. That's the secret to this loaf, which has maximum personality through minimum work.

The personality in this instance is emphatically Spanish. To that end, make sure that you buy Spanish and not Mexican chorizo, in the form of a thick baton, not thin slices, as you want to dice it into tiny cubes, a textural delight in the cooked loaf. Chorizo is dry and firm enough to be diced easily with a sharp knife; the same holds true for the Manchego cheese, which should not be shredded conventionally.

If you're a heat-lover, seize the option of adding red pepper; if you're wary, rest assured that the chorizo and the smoked paprika provide ample oomph. Because this loaf is an especially tender one that slices delicately, make the mixture two to four hours in advance, if you can, and put it in the refrigerator, then take it out and form it into a loaf only when you're ready to put it in the oven.

Slice the loaf carefully, to keep each moist portion intact.

1 cup uncooked long-grain white rice

½ teaspoon salt

1 pound ground pork

½ pound dry Spanish chorizo, diced into ⅓-inch cubes

9–10 ounces Manchego cheese, similarly diced

4 eggs, lightly beaten

3 tablespoons tomato paste

2 cloves garlic, minced

1 teaspoon smoked Spanish paprika

½ teaspoon red pepper flakes or other red pepper (optional)

1. Preheat the oven to 350 degrees F. Line a 9-by-13-inch (or larger) baking pan with nonstick aluminum foil.

2. Cook the rice in accordance with the package directions, stirring the salt into the water before it comes to a boil. As soon as the rice is done, measure out 2 cups (not too tightly packed) and place that in a large mixing bowl; allow it to cool a bit. Fluff the rice with a fork.

3. Once the rice has cooled some, add the pork, chorizo, cheese, eggs, tomato paste, garlic, paprika and red pepper flakes (if using), and mix very thoroughly with your clean hands, pressing and kneading the mixture with considerable force for several minutes to soften the pork.

4. Transfer the mixture to the prepared baking dish and shape it into a thick loaf that runs almost the entire length of the dish but leaves at least an inch of room on each side. Cook for 55 minutes or until

the internal temperature is 160 degrees F. Remove the pan from the oven and let the loaf rest, uncovered, for 10 minutes. Then slice it into individual portions and serve.

Chicken Curry Masala Loaf with Mango Chutney Glaze

Serves 4 generously

Chicken curry is, at this point in American life, a form of vernacular comfort food. It's also the gateway entree to Indian dining, ordered by college students who scarf it down before a marathon of *The Walking Dead*. It is the entry-level office worker's sack lunch, in the form of leftovers, or perhaps as a salad. And it is the mainstay of the Indian buffet, consumed at some point by all of us on a first date.

Given our mutual love of the dish, we wondered about its interpretation in a meatloaf. A chicken loaf, that is. Actual curry powder lacked the heat and complexity to stand up to ground meat, but garam masala did the trick. The oats are a terrific binder and the peas provide a lovely dash of color. We like heat and add some chile, but you don't have to. The chutney gives it a sweet finish.

LOAF

1 tablespoon olive oil

⅓ cup diced onion

3 cloves garlic, finely chopped

1 large egg

1 tablespoon tomato paste

2 teaspoons garam masala

1¼ teaspoons salt

1 inch fresh ginger, grated

½ cup quick-cooking oats

1½ pounds ground chicken

½ cup chopped fresh cilantro or flat-leaf parsley leaves

½ cup chopped peeled green apple

½ cup frozen peas, thawed

½ cup cubed cooked sweet potato (boiled only until just tender)

½ serrano chile, finely chopped (unless your mango chutney contains chiles; optional)

GLAZE

1 cup mango chutney (store-bought unless you make your own, which is awesome—good for you!)

1. Preheat the oven to 350 degrees F. Line a 9-by-13-inch baking pan with aluminum foil or parchment paper.

2. Heat the oil in a medium-sized skillet over low heat, add the onions and sauté until soft, about 7 minutes. Add the garlic and cook for another 2 minutes. Remove the pan from the heat and let cool.

3. In a medium-sized bowl, beat the egg, tomato paste, garam masala, salt and ginger with a fork. Then stir in the oats and let the mixture sit for about 10 minutes.

4. Stir the onions and the ground chicken into the oat mixture. Then, using a spoon, fold in the cilantro or parsley, apples, peas, sweet potatoes and chile (if using). Form the mixture into a loaf in the prepared baking pan, tapering the ends, making them narrower.

5. To make the glaze, puree the chutney in a food processor or blender until it forms a sticky paste. Spread the puree over the loaf from end to end.

6. Bake for about 40 minutes or until the internal temperature reaches 160 degrees F. Let sit ten minutes lightly tented with foil, then slice and serve.

Swedish Meatball Loaf

For so many of us, the best part of trips to IKEA comes after the trek around the store in search of difficult-to-assemble (but incredibly cheap!) particleboard beds and primary-colored bathmats. That's when we retire to the cafe and avail ourselves of those little, completely uniform meatballs smothered in cream sauce and topped with traditional lingonberry jam.

We're clearly not alone. The company sells 1 billion meatballs a year across 360 locations in 47 countries. We've translated those balls into a loaf with all the traditional components: beef and pork; bread that's swelled in cream; a fruity topping. To combine the ingredients in the loaf, we use a standing mixer, which gives Swedish meatballs a bouncy texture of sorts and does the same for our loaf. The loaf will shrink quite a bit in the oven. Expect that and don't worry about it.

The gravy comes from a traditional roux with equal parts fat and flour, and we top it with something sweet. If you can locate lingonberries, knock yourself out. We found raspberry jam to be a sublime substitute, and it's what really brings the dish together.

LOAF

> 1 large egg
>
> ½ cup heavy cream
>
> 2 cups cubed white bread
>
> 2 teaspoons neutral oil, such as vegetable oil
>
> 1 small onion, diced
>
> 1 pound ground pork
>
> 1 pound ground beef
>
> ½ teaspoon ground allspice
>
> ¼ teaspoon grated nutmeg
>
> 1 tablespoon kosher salt
>
> ¼ teaspoon freshly ground black pepper

GRAVY

> 4 tablespoons (½ stick) unsalted butter
>
> 4 tablespoons all-purpose flour
>
> 2⅔ cups beef broth
>
> ½ cup heavy cream
>
> ⅓ cup sour cream
>
> 2 teaspoons Worcestershire sauce
>
> ¼ teaspoon freshly ground black pepper
>
> 1 tablespoon fresh lemon juice

TOPPING

> Raspberry jam
>
> Roughly chopped fresh parsley (optional)

FOR THE LOAF

1. Preheat the oven to 325 degrees F. Line a rimmed baking sheet with aluminum foil or parchment paper.

2. Whisk the egg and cream together in a medium-sized bowl. Add the bread cubes and set the bowl aside.

3. Warm the oil in a small saucepan over medium-low heat, add the onions and sauté until they are soft, about 7 minutes.

4. In a standing mixer fitted with the paddle attachment, beat the pork, beef, allspice, nutmeg, salt and pepper on high speed, scraping the bowl as necessary, until the mixture is smooth and pale, about

2 minutes. Add the bread mixture and sautéed onions and beat on low speed until combined, about 3 minutes.

5. Remove the mixture and use your clean hands to form it into a loaf on the prepared baking sheet. Bake in the oven for about 45 minutes or until the internal temperature reaches 155 degrees F.

FOR THE GRAVY

1. While your meatloaf cooks, melt the butter in a large saucepan over medium-high heat. Add the flour and whisk constantly for about 2 minutes.

2. Mix in the broth, whisking away any lumps, and bring to a boil. Reduce the heat to medium and cook, whisking now and then, until the sauce has thickened, about 10 minutes.

3. Add the heavy cream, sour cream, Worcestershire sauce and pepper and bring to a boil.

4. Reduce the heat to medium and cook until the sauce is thick enough to coat a spoon, about 10 minutes. Stir in the lemon juice, and adjust the seasoning if necessary.

TO FINISH

1. Remove the baking sheet from the oven and let the meatloaf rest, uncovered, for 10 minutes.

2. Slice the loaf, and cover each piece with some gravy and a dollop of raspberry jam. If you have it, sprinkle some parsley on top.

South African Bobotie Loaf

This isn't a meatloaf per se, because it's actually cooked in a casserole dish. But bobotie, a dish of minced meat that's married to South Asian spices and baked with an egg-custard topping, is often referred to as the meatloaf of South Africa.

The first time we made it, the flavors were divine but we were sad to see the topping disappear into the meat. The solution, suggested by an obsessive tester whom we recruited, was to drain the fat from the meat after sautéing it, and to double the amount of bread and to use some cream. Delicious! And lovely to look at.

Final note: Chutney can be spicy, and that's to be expected. If you want even more heat, add a bit of cayenne. If you are using preserves, the result will be much sweeter.

LOAF

½ cup whole milk

½ cup half-and-half

4 bay leaves

4 slices white sandwich bread (with crusts), torn into large pieces

2 tablespoons vegetable oil

1 medium onion, finely chopped

2 small cloves garlic, minced

2 pounds ground lamb

1 Granny Smith apple, peeled, cored and finely chopped

1 ounce Asian tamarind paste

1 tablespoon curry powder

2 tablespoons apricot preserves or chutney

3 tablespoons golden raisins

½ cup slivered almonds

1 tablespoon kosher salt

½ teaspoon freshly ground black pepper

TOPPING

2 eggs

⅛ teaspoon freshly grated nutmeg

1 teaspoon grated lemon zest

1. Preheat the oven to 325 degrees F. Lightly oil a 2-quart baking dish.

2. Heat the milk and half-and-half in a saucepan until bubbles form around the edge. Remove the pan from the heat and add the bay leaves. Set aside for 10 minutes. Then remove the bay leaves and add the bread pieces. Set pan aside.

3. In a large sauté pan over low heat, heat the oil. Add the onions and cook until they are translucent and fragrant, about 10 minutes. Add the garlic and cook for another 2 minutes.

4. Add the lamb to the pan, breaking it up and cooking until it is no longer pink, about five minutes. With a large spoon, remove the excess fat from the pan. Add the apples, tamarind paste, curry powder, preserves or chutney, raisins, almonds, salt and pepper. Cook until the apples have softened—about 4 minutes.

5. Squeeze all the milk you can from the bread, reserving the milk in a small bowl. Add the bread to the mixture in the sauté pan. Stir to combine, and then pour the mixture into the prepared baking dish. Set it aside.

6. To make the topping, add the eggs, nutmeg and lemon zest to the reserved milk, and beat until frothy. Pour this over the meat mixture.

7. Bake for 35 to 40 minutes, until the top is bubbling and browning.

8. Remove the dish from the oven and let the bobotie cool for about 10 minutes before spooning it out and serving.

Japanese Loaf with Miso and Mirin

Serves 6

This loaf was inspired by yakitori, the Japanese skewered chicken, which is generally grilled and often basted with a sweet sauce. The goal here was to use a meat that is less lean than chicken, for a more flavorful loaf, while retaining and enhancing the best qualities of the original dish. A combination of turkey and pork did the trick.

Our first attempt at this loaf, while interesting, lacked the layers of flavors found in the skewer and was a bit too one-dimensional, like eating the interior meat of a soup dumpling while still longing for the dumpling shell or the soup. The key was an additional flavor—ginger, to be precise—and a *tare* glaze that is essentially a riff on the sauce generally used with yakitori. The loaf as tweaked by our friend Linda, a fabulous cook with an intense imagination, retains that very bound texture of a dumpling interior or skewered meatball, but with a great depth of flavor, like a soup.

She served it with a roasted broccoli, garlic and peanut mixture with a honey-soy-Sriracha sauce. We also recommend Sam Molavi's Wow Brussels Sprouts (page 240). Once you assemble all the ingredients, it takes about ten minutes to prep the glaze, and you can make the loaf mixture while the glaze is doing its thing on the stove.

TARE GLAZE

½ cup mirin

⅓ cup soy sauce

¼ cup sake

¼ cup packed dark brown sugar

2 tablespoons sherry vinegar

3 cloves garlic, smashed

1 inch fresh ginger, sliced

1 tablespoon whole black peppercorns (optional; omit if you dislike
    this texture)

LOAF

1 pound ground turkey

½ pound ground pork

1 tablespoon white miso paste

1 tablespoon soy sauce

1 tablespoon mirin

2 teaspoons toasted sesame oil

1 tablespoon grated fresh ginger (from a thumb-sized piece)

2 cloves garlic, minced

1 large egg

1 cup panko bread crumbs

½ teaspoon ground white pepper

4 scallions (white parts), finely minced,
    plus extra chopped scallion for garnish

1 tablespoon sesame seeds

1. Make the glaze by placing all the ingredients in a small saucepan and bringing them to a boil. Then reduce the heat and simmer for 30 minutes, until the glaze is reduced and coats the back of a spoon. Strain the glaze through a fine-mesh strainer into a measuring cup. You should have about 1 cup of glaze.

2. Meanwhile, heat the oven to 350 degrees F. Line a rimmed baking sheet with parchment paper.

3. Place the turkey and pork in the bowl of a standing mixer or in a large mixing bowl.

4. In a small bowl or measuring cup, whisk together the miso paste, soy sauce, mirin and sesame oil until the miso paste is completely incorporated; pour this over the meats.

5. Add the ginger, garlic, egg, panko, white pepper and minced scallions to the meats, and mix on low speed until incorporated (2 minutes or so); or mix it well with your clean hands. Place the meat mixture on the prepared baking sheet and shape it into a loaf.

6. Brush the loaf with the tare glaze and bake it in the oven, basting it with the glaze every 20 minutes, until the internal temperature reaches 160 degrees F, about 1 hour. Remove the baking sheet from the oven and let the meatloaf rest, uncovered, for 10 minutes.

7. Brush the loaf one more time with the tare glaze, and sprinkle it with the sesame seeds and chopped scallions. Slice and serve.

lamb-colored glasses

THREE

Lamb

Frank: And now we come to the meat that I love best in our various
loaves. The meat that I can't promote strenuously enough. The meat
that I can't abide any disagreement over. While I abhor excessive
partisanship and tribalism in politics, I endorse it in food, and I
could and would spend the rest of my life in a land of only lamb-
lovers, where the national dish is leg of lamb and the national
anthem is "Mary Had a Little Lamb." Did I mention that one of my
all-time favorite movies is *The Silence of the Lambs?*

Jenn: I think you didn't get enough sleep last night. Maybe you should
count sheep. It's interesting: Lamb has such a distinct flavor, you'd
think it would compete with seasonings, glazes and the like. But just
as a black dress is the vehicle for all things sexy, sophisticated and
embellished, lamb is a protean protein that showcases all manner of
spices and flavors. Lamb puts the love in curry. It brings out the best
in something subtle like sumac. It bear-hugs intense heat but is also
happy to air-kiss something mild-mannered like yogurt or pine nuts.
Although we spend this entire chapter on just one fleecy mammal,

we rummage through an entire pantry—and traverse the globe—as we do.

Frank: Really, we could have called this chapter "Around the World," or rather "Around the World on a Lamb." Several of these loaves—especially the Meatloaf with Moroccan Flair (page 100), the Jerusalem Loaf with Sumac and Couscous (page 104) and Mike Solomonov's Spicy Merguez Loaf (page 110)—beautifully illustrate all the truths you just told about lamb as the perfect playdate for a riot of strong and exotic flourishes. Speaking of Solomonov, do you know his whole backstory?

Jenn: Fill me in. I love his restaurant Zahav in Philadelphia.

Frank: That's a special place, devoted to Israeli cooking and just one of his many terrific Philly spots. It's also a triumph of resilience and recovery. To backtrack: Mike and his brother grew up in both the United States and Israel, and when his brother was in his last days of compulsory service in the Israeli military, he was shot and killed by sniper fire along the Lebanese border. After that, Mike fell into a dark period, abusing drugs and becoming a crack cocaine addict. It almost derailed his budding restaurant career. But his business partner and his wife staged an intervention, and now he's among the most closely watched chefs nationwide, with expansion plans and a cookbook of his own, *Zahav: A World of Israeli Cooking*, that was published in late 2015 to enormous acclaim.

Jenn: What a classic, poignant reminder of how the kitchen becomes salvation for so many. He's such a nice guy—when we told him that it was just about impossible to find the Aleppo pepper that the recipe he gave us called for, on account of, you know, the war in Aleppo, and asked if we could please use something else in this fantastic and wholly unique meatloaf, he instantly said, "Okay." (For points of surly contrast, we refer readers to *Top Chef*—pick your season.) His loaf, as readers will discover, uses very interesting techniques and spices to essentially make a sausage, a sausage with a surprise. Meatloaf is such a great vehicle for "Hey, who knew?" especially when it comes to the world of binders. For instance, our Kibbeh Loaf with Pine Nuts (page 107), a tribute to that beloved staple of Lebanese cooking, uses bulgur to bring the lamb and seasonings together. Who knew?

Frank: We could have called this book *Meatloaf: Who Knew?*

Jenn: Again, *take a sleeping pill*. Meantime, let's talk about lamb and its roadshow buddy, mint. Mint shows up frequently in this chapter, replacing parsley as the herb of choice for many ground meat dishes. What I find interesting about mint is that while it's flamboyantly fragrant when it's lolling around the good old cutting board, it becomes all demure in meat. You need a lot of it to bring out its springtime swagger.

Frank: I totally agree. Until this book, I never fully appreciated mint or especially the mint-lamb nexus, which I associated with my father's unconscionable use of mint jelly on lamb chops. I now cut him more slack, although I still oppose the *jellying* of mint. As for lamb chops, I would like to seize this opportunity to plug the "legendary mutton chop"—that's how it's listed on the menu—at Keens Steakhouse in Manhattan. It's really not mutton. It's lamb that's a bit more mature than the culinary norm. Think lamb with a driver's license. Lamb that's been to the prom. Again I'm wandering off topic, but this chapter is my shining moment of lamb evangelism. I'm packing in as much lamb scripture and as many lamb homilies as I can.

Jenn: Remember that episode of *Seinfeld* in which Elaine carried a mutton chop around in her purse and got attacked by a dog? Or was it George?

Frank: George who carried the mutton chop? Or George who attacked Elaine? Are you sure that Kramer wasn't involved somehow? I can see him with a mutton chop *and* with a purse.

Jenn: No, it was Elaine. Definitely Elaine. That's sort of my mutton mental moment. And I hope you noted and silently complimented me on my alliteration just then. I want to flag another dalliance of mint and lamb, which actually have a three-way with some cilantro in April Bloomfield's Lamb Loaf with Yogurt and Mint (page 96), in which much of the flavor comes not from the loaf itself but from the sauce.

Frank: April's another phenomenally talented chef, and both she and Mike in their various restaurants traffic heavily in lamb. That's proof of their genius, though I tend to see the world through lamb-colored glasses. Back when I reviewed restaurants, the bloggers who analyzed and deconstructed my weekly appraisals—yes, such bloggers exist!—apparently quantified and commented on my lamb-loving predilections.

Jenn: So in summary: lamb. We like it very much. To do right by it, we suggest that readers have curry powder in the larder. The chefs featured here would also prefer that home cooks grind their own meat. We have a more realistic view of the world, and understand that our readers have jobs and children and Amazon carts that need pruning and crazy eye doctors who keep sending the same bill over and over again. But we would urge readers, when serving lamb, to invite guests. Guests love lamb.

Greek Loaf with Lamb and Feta

This meatloaf has surprise atop surprise. It's an embarrassment of indulgences.

In addition to the lamb, with its robust flavor and perfect (for meatloaf) degree of fattiness, there's feta, the tang and creaminess of which make a real statement.

And then: pine nuts. We love pine nuts, which you don't see and eat every day, or even every week, in part because you can't afford to. They're expensive. But they deepen this meatloaf's sense of place, its redolence of sunbaked countries in the southern Mediterranean.

We've built a couple of options into this recipe. You can scale the feta up or down depending on your appetite for it and how much you crave a softer, creamier meatloaf. You can scale the pine nuts up or down based on your budget and your fondness for them.

Do not substitute dried herbs for the fresh rosemary and fresh mint, the latter of which is crucial here. It brightens and sharpens the flavors in an ideal way. Eating this meatloaf, with its minty top notes, we understood for the first time why some people pair mint jelly with their lamb chops, though we plan never to do that ourselves. We're just not mint-jelly types.

2 tablespoons olive oil

1½ small onions, finely chopped (about ¾ cup)

3 cloves garlic, minced

½–¾ cup pine nuts

½–¾ cup whole milk

3 thick slices white bread, crusts removed

1½ pounds ground lamb

6–8 ounces Greek feta cheese, crumbled

½ cup chopped fresh mint leaves

3 tablespoons minced fresh rosemary leaves

2 eggs, lightly beaten

3 tablespoons tomato paste

3 teaspoons Worcestershire sauce

⅔ teaspoon coarsely ground black pepper

Pint- or quart-sized container of store-bought tzatziki

  (a yogurt, cucumber and dill sauce)

1. Preheat the oven to 250 degrees F. Spray a rimmed baking sheet with cooking oil. Line a 9-by-13-inch (or larger) baking dish with nonstick aluminum foil.

2. Use enough of the olive oil to thinly coat a small or medium-sized skillet, and cook the onions and garlic over medium heat, stirring occasionally, until they soften and the onions turn somewhat translucent, about 10 minutes.

3. Meanwhile, spread the pine nuts on the prepared baking sheet, and toast them lightly in the oven for 10 to 12 minutes, until their color darkens

significantly and their aroma blooms—but remove them before they turn fully brown. Turn the oven temperature up to 350 degrees F.

4. Pour the milk into a shallow bowl and dredge the slices of bread through it, fully moistening each side. Then transfer the bread to a large mixing bowl, tearing it into small pieces.

5. Add the onion mixture, pine nuts, lamb, feta, mint, rosemary, eggs, tomato paste, Worcestershire and pepper to the bread in the large bowl. With your clean hands, mix everything together so that the ingredients are distributed evenly.

6. Transfer the mixture to the prepared baking dish and shape it into a loaf with a consistent width and slightly narrower, tapered ends. Bake for 55 minutes, or to 145 degrees F for medium.

7. Remove the baking dish from the oven and let the meatloaf rest, uncovered, for 10 to 15 minutes before slicing, drizzling the slices with tzatziki and serving.

April Bloomfield's Lamb Loaf with Yogurt and Mint

C all it deconstructed meatloaf. For this recipe, April Bloomfield, the British chef with two New York–based Michelin-starred restaurants under her toque, takes you on a tour of her professional mind and kitchen. Here she has developed a lamb meatloaf that gets the lion's share of its flavor—rich Middle Eastern spices, piquant chile peppers and delightfully acidic tomatoes—not from the loaf but from the sauce.

For the meatloaf, April says, you want to use light, airy, delicate ground meat, which is why she prefers to grind it herself. We will leave that step as optional for those of you watching at home (but we do include instructions for at-home grinding below). Either way, April stresses that the Maldon salt is the key to the meatloaf's success. She has some additional tricks, like blending half of the sauce halfway through the cooking process; this improves its structure. While the sauce simmers slowly on the stove, she warns, "I always freak out at this point because the sauce seems so bland, but don't worry—it'll taste amazing after you're done." We agree.

LOAF

2½ pounds boneless lamb shoulder, ground (see Note)

2½ tablespoons Maldon or another flaky sea salt

2 cups fine, unseasoned bread crumbs

SAUCE

1 tablespoon extra-virgin
olive oil

1 large Spanish onion,
finely chopped

5 cloves garlic, thinly sliced

½ teaspoon Maldon
or another flaky sea salt

2 teaspoons coriander seeds, toasted and ground

1½ teaspoons cumin seeds, toasted and ground

2 dried, long spicy red chiles, pierced with a sharp knife

1 28-ounce can peeled whole tomatoes, drained, trimmed and
squished with your hands

GARNISH

About ½ cup plain full-fat Greek-style yogurt

A small handful of fresh mint leaves

A small handful of small, delicate cilantro sprigs

Extra-virgin olive oil (for cooking optional eggs)

Fried eggs (optional)

FOR THE LOAF

1. Preheat the oven to 400 degrees F.

2. In a large bowl, toss the ground lamb well with the salt; then add the bread crumbs and toss again. Take the mixture and form it into a loaf shape in a medium-sized roasting pan, with room around it for the sauce.

FOR THE SAUCE

1. Heat the oil in a medium-sized Dutch oven over medium-high heat. Add the onions, garlic and salt and cook, stirring often, until the onions are soft and lightly browned and the garlic smells toasty and is a deep golden brown, about 5 minutes. Add the coriander, cumin and chiles and cook for 1 minute, stirring constantly.

2. Turn the heat to low, add the tomatoes and simmer gently until the tomatoes begin to stick to the bottom of the pot, about 10 minutes.

3. Add 4 cups of water and raise the heat to bring the sauce to a boil; then turn it down to maintain a gentle simmer and cook for 5 minutes more. Transfer 2 cups of the sauce to a blender, give it a whiz until it's smooth and airy and stir it back into the sauce in the pot. Simmer for 5 more minutes.

4. Pour the sauce over and around the meatloaf, and cover with aluminum foil. Cook for 1 hour. Then remove the foil and cook for an additional 10 to 15 minutes, until the meatloaf is lightly browned and the internal temperature reaches 160 degrees F. Remove the roasting pan from the oven and let the meatloaf rest, uncovered, for 10 minutes.

5. To serve, place a slice of meatloaf on a plate and ladle some sauce over it. Add a blob of yogurt to the plate, and sprinkle the yogurt with

mint leaves and cilantro. Serve with a fried egg if you like, and eat straightaway.

Note: *If you are grinding your own meat, place the lamb in a large mixing bowl, cover the bowl with plastic wrap, and pop it in the freezer until the edges get crunchy, about 1 hour. Cover the lamb well with the salt; then add the bread crumbs and toss again. Using the meat grinder attachment of a standing mixer, grind the mixture through a medium die into a bowl twice; then form into a loaf.*

The chefs who contributed to this cookbook weren't asked for specific recipes; we wanted them to follow their hearts. When we received **April Bloomfield's Lamb Loaf with Yogurt and Mint**, we were especially thrilled, because one of her classics is the lamb burger at her Manhattan restaurant The Breslin. Its construction works perfectly for leftovers of her lamb loaf. Sear a slice of it in a skillet with a neutral cooking oil or quickly grill it. Put a thin square of feta over that, along with raw onion (optional). Use a big ciabatta-style bun. Dress it lightly with mayonnaise that has cumin mixed into it. This same treatment works for the **Meatloaf with Moroccan Flair** (page 100).

Meatloaf with Moroccan Flair

This loaf is the invention of our dear friend Anne Kornblut, who developed it while learning to cook new dishes with her beloved babysitter, Mary, in California, where the freshest of herbs can be found year-round.

"We were combining our various heritage backgrounds—Afghan, Jewish, Italian, Costa Rican, Berkeley—to come up with all sorts of dishes," Anne said. "We thought of Moroccan meatloaf after we learned how to do shakshuka one month and were in a Moroccan frame of mind."

We confess that when we first read this recipe, we worried that the plethora of spices and large amounts of garlic would be overwhelming. *Hellllloooooo*, twelve cloves of garlic! But Anne understood what meatloaf-ers all come to know: Ground meat has a deep tolerance for seasoning, and indeed is usually improved by it. The sheer greenness of the herbs is an excellent foil for all the rich seasonings, and the veggies give this loaf an especially lovely texture.

1 tablespoon olive oil

1 onion, diced

12 garlic cloves, minced

3 stalks celery, diced (about ½ cup)

1 large carrot, peeled and diced (about ½ cup)

3 inches fresh ginger, minced (about ⅓ cup)

1 tablespoon ground cinnamon

2 tablespoons ground cumin

1 tablespoon ground coriander

2 tablespoons smoked paprika

1 teaspoon salt

7 tablespoons tomato paste

½ cup chopped fresh cilantro leaves

½ cup chopped fresh mint leaves

½ cup chopped fresh parsley leaves

2 eggs, lightly beaten

1 cup whole-wheat unseasoned bread crumbs

2 pounds ground lamb

SIDE SAUCE (OPTIONAL)

1 cup plain full-fat Greek-style yogurt

3 tablespoons fresh lemon juice

½ cup pine nuts, toasted in a 375 degree F oven until fragrant and golden brown (about 7 minutes)

1. Preheat the oven to 350 degrees F.
2. Heat the olive oil in a large pan, and once it's hot, toss in the onions. Stir for 5 minutes. Add the garlic and stir for another minute or two. Then add the celery, carrots and ginger and cook for about 5 minutes,

adding more olive oil as needed to make sure the ingredients are well coated and softening.

3. Next, add the spices: cinnamon, cumin, coriander, smoked paprika and salt. Stir them into the mixture well. Lastly, add the tomato paste. Cook for another 5 minutes, stirring well. (You can alter the spices here to your liking, adding more or less of those recommended or adding curry powder, nutmeg, allspice, black pepper or cayenne.)

4. Once the mixture is cooked, remove the pan from the heat and let it cool for about 15 minutes.

5. While it cools, combine the fresh herbs—cilantro, mint and parsley—with the eggs and bread crumbs in a large bowl. Then add the ground lamb and the cooled mixture of onion, garlic, spices and tomato paste. Mix well with your clean hands until all ingredients are blended.

6. Place the meat mixture into a loaf pan and cover with aluminum foil. Then create a water bath by placing the loaf pan into a larger baking pan and filling the larger pan halfway with water. (This bath helps keep the meatloaf from drying out by keeping the temperature more even during baking.)

7. Put the meatloaf, in the bath, into the oven and cook for approximately 1 hour 30 minutes. After an hour, check the meatloaf, and remove the foil cover if you would like a firmer top to the loaf. Bake until the internal temperature reaches 140 degrees F.

8. Remove the pan from the oven, lift the loaf pan out of the water bath and let the meatloaf rest, uncovered, for at least 5 minutes. If there is excessive grease, which will depend on how fatty the meat was, you can carefully pour that out.

9. Serve warm, at room temperature, or cooled, depending on your taste.

10. For the sauce, mix the yogurt, lemon juice and pine nuts together, and serve in a small dish on the side.

Jerusalem Loaf with Sumac and Couscous

Serves 5

This recipe is inspired by the divine lamb meatballs with barberries from *Jerusalem: A Cookbook*, by Yotam Ottolenghi and Sami Tamimi, which is now pretty much a cult classic for home cooks interested in Middle Eastern food. The key is lamb with fruit, though we have substituted their barberries (would we do that to you?) with dried cranberries, and we've carefully chosen spices and herbs that capture the sensibility of the sauce that they use to steep the meatballs. These accents bring the earthiness of the lamb into relief and take you on a fragrant mental (and gustatory) journey across the ocean. Our binder here is in clever keeping with the ethnic spirit: Israeli couscous, also known as pearl couscous, which can be found in most grocery stores. We suggest a dollop of yogurt on top.

1 tablespoon olive oil

1 large yellow onion, chopped

⅓ cup chopped shallots

1⅔ pounds ground lamb

1 cup cooked Israeli couscous, prepared according to the package directions

2 large eggs

2 cloves garlic, sliced thin

⅓ cup mixed chopped fresh mint, tarragon, dill and cilantro

¾ teaspoon ground allspice

¾ teaspoon ground cumin

Scant ¼ teaspoon ground sumac

1 teaspoon salt

1 teaspoon freshly ground black pepper

⅔ cup dried cranberries

Plain full-fat non-Greek yogurt, for serving (optional)

1. Preheat the oven to 350 degrees F. Line a large baking sheet with aluminum foil.

2. Heat the oil in a medium-sized skillet, add the onions and shallots and sauté until fragrant and soft, about 10 minutes. Remove from the heat and let cool.

3. In the meantime, combine all the remaining ingredients, except the yogurt, in a large bowl. When the onions are slightly cool, add them to the meat mix. With your clean hands, form a loaf on the prepared baking sheet, even in shape but narrowed at each end.

4. Bake in the oven for 50 minutes or until the interior is pink and the internal temperature reaches 155 degrees F. Remove the baking sheet from the oven and let the loaf rest, uncovered, for 10 minutes before slicing. Serve with dollops of yogurt, if desired.

tomorrow's LUNCH

It's pita time. Heat or even sear leftovers of our **Greek Loaf** with **Lamb and Feta** (page 93), our **Kibbeh Loaf with Pine Nuts** (page 107) or Mike Solomonov's **Spicy Merguez Loaf** (page 110) and then tuck the meat, sliced or crumbled, into a generously sized pita pocket with diced or thinly sliced cucumber, diced tomato and some kind of garlic-yogurt (like tzatziki) or tahini sauce for an eat-on-the-go treat that evokes the best halal food carts in New York.

Kibbeh Loaf with Pine Nuts

Serves 4

his is our take on a famous Lebanese dish fashioned from bulgur, minced onions and ground lean beef, lamb or even goat. (Also, apparently, sometimes camel.) Various North African and Middle Eastern countries do versions of kibbeh (also spelled kibbe, kibbah and a few more ways, just to keep things confusing), which is often served as a canapé or appetizer, alternates between round and oval and can be smaller or larger: a golf ball in the hands of some cooks, a flying saucer in the hands of others. In our hands, it's a meatloaf—and a respectable dinner in its own right.

This loaf gets its special perfume from Middle Eastern spices, which amplify the earthiness of the bulgur. We found that it was brightened by Aleppo pepper (which is sadly hard to find these days, due to the conflict in Syria) and a bevy of herbs. At first we just went with a modest dose of mint, which can get lost in ground meat, but for the next go-round we boosted the amount and added parsley for an extra measure of vegetal freshness. Bingo. But show some restraint when eating this, or maybe upsize the recipe, because this loaf is excellent reheated the next day.

1 tablespoon olive oil

½ cup diced onion

1 large onion, sliced thin

1 pound ground lamb

1 cup coarse-ground bulgur, rinsed and soaked in cold water for 20 minutes, then drained

1 teaspoon freshly ground black pepper

½ teaspoon ground allspice

1½ teaspoons ground cumin

1 teaspoon ground cinnamon

1 teaspoon hot paprika or Aleppo pepper

1 tablespoon salt

½ cup chopped fresh mint leaves

¼ cup chopped fresh parsley leaves

½ cup pine nuts, toasted in a 375 degree F oven until fragrant and golden brown (about 7 minutes)

Plain full-fat Greek-style yogurt, for serving (optional)

1. Preheat the oven to 350 degrees F. Line a large rimmed baking sheet with aluminum foil or parchment paper.
2. Heat the oil in a medium-sized pan over medium heat. Add the diced onions and sauté until soft, about 10 minutes. Remove from the pan and set aside to cool.
3. Turn the heat to low, add the onion slices to the pan and sauté until soft, 10 minutes or so. (If you keep the heat low enough, you can sauté them as long as you'd like.)

4. In the meantime, combine the lamb, bulgur, spices, salt and herbs in a large bowl. Add the cooled diced onions and combine gently with your clean hands until just mixed. Form the mixture into a loaf on the prepared baking sheet. Cover it with the softened onion slices and toasted pine nuts.

5. Bake for 40 minutes or until the internal temperature reaches 150 degrees F for medium-rare or 160 degrees F for medium. Remove the baking sheet from the oven and let the meatloaf rest, uncovered, for 10 minutes before slicing and serving, with a dollop of yogurt on the side if you like.

Mike Solomonov's Spicy Merguez Loaf

Serves 4

Mike Solomonov, the chef at the acclaimed Philadelphia restaurant Zahav, brings us a loaf with flavors so complex and elements so varied that your guests will presume you spent hours standing over your stove, rocking out to Green Day and stirring. If you choose to make the optional harissa ketchup featured here, rather than purchasing commercial harissa, they will be partially correct.

But in truth, in the time-to-benefit ratio, this dish is the greatest boon to your meatloaf-ing life. You can mix up the loaf in about five minutes, as there is minimal chopping. It then develops its flavors and texture in the fridge while you sleep, go to work, spend the entire day secretly praying that one of your colleagues is transferred to Manila, leave work, curse traffic, stop at the store for some much-needed red wine and race into the house to finish the dish.

You will find the loaf batter drier than others you have made, because it is indeed sausage-like. This loaf's calling card is its fire—both in the loaf and in the glaze—so it's for those who like it hot. We give you an alternative to the Aleppo pepper that Mike says is ideal to use, because Aleppo's availability is limited due to conflicts in Syria, home of, yes, Aleppo. When slicing this loaf, use a bit of extra elbow grease to get through the surprising (and delightful) boiled eggs. The chef recommends a loaf pan here, and we agree, although if you don't own one it will work well on a baking sheet lined with parchment paper.

FOR THE MERGUEZ

> 1 pound ground lamb
>
> 1 tablespoon ground cumin
>
> 1 tablespoon ground coriander
>
> 1 tablespoon ground caraway
>
> 1 tablespoon ground cardamom
>
> 2 tablespoons ground fennel
>
> 2 tablespoons Aleppo pepper or hot or smoked paprika (not sweet)
>
> 1 tablespoon sugar
>
> 4 tablespoons kosher salt
>
> ½ cup chopped fresh parsley
>
> ½ cup chopped fresh cilantro
>
> 2 tablespoons minced garlic
>
> 2 tablespoons tahini sauce or paste
>
>> (different brands label it differently)
>
> 1 cup harissa (store-bought or see recipe below)
>
> 1 cup torn challah bread
>
> 4 hard-boiled eggs, peeled, ends trimmed off
>
> 12 pitted black olives, cut in half

HARISSA KETCHUP (optional alternative to store-bought harissa)

> 1 cup Aleppo peppers (or easier-to-find serranos), seeded
>
> 6 tablespoons white vinegar

3 tablespoons brown sugar

2 tablespoons minced garlic

1 cup tomato paste

2 tablespoons salt

1 tablespoon ground cumin

1 tablespoon ground coriander

SUPER FANCY

1 jar grape leaves, rinsed

1. In a large bowl, combine the lamb with the spices, sugar, salt, parsley, cilantro, garlic and tahini. Mix thoroughly with your clean hands, cover and refrigerate for 12 to 24 hours.

2. If you are making your own harissa ketchup, combine all of its ingredients with 1 cup of water in a small pot and cook over medium-low heat, stirring occasionally, until quite thick, roughly 30 minutes. Once it has thickened, puree it in a food processor or blender until creamy but not watery.

3. Put half of the homemade harissa ketchup or of the store-bought harissa into a medium-sized bowl and stir in the challah pieces with a spoon. Knead this into the meatloaf mixture and put it all back in the fridge for 10 more minutes.

4. Now would be a good time to turn on your oven, to 350 degrees F.

5. If you are using the grape leaves, line a terrine or loaf pan with those grape leaves. Otherwise skip this step.

6. Place half of the meatloaf mixture in the loaf pan, and arrange the hard-boiled eggs lengthwise in a line down the center. Scatter the olives between and around the eggs. Place the rest of the meatloaf mixture over the eggs, pressing it down lightly to cover them.

7. Slather the top of the loaf with the rest of the harissa.

8. Bake for about 45 minutes, until the internal temperature reaches 160 degrees F.

9. Allow the loaf to rest for 10 minutes in the pan; then remove from the pan, slice and serve.

Cluck Cluck, Gobble Gobble

Jenn: People have strong feelings about poultry, and often they are not very warm. Turkey is maligned outside the Thanksgiving table as a meat best left for grade-school lunches, and chicken, while embraced in certain situations, is shunned when it's ground. It's considered a flavorless vessel for those who put their waistlines before their taste buds.

Frank: I have never put my waistline before my taste buds, as is sadly evident, and I'm not reversing that decision or revising that sensibility. I have, however, changed my feelings about ground turkey and ground chicken, inasmuch as the meatloaves that we developed here are among my favorites in the book. They're lessons in how you adjust for the lesser fat content and subtler flavor of poultry. One of those lessons: Use ground dark meat when possible.

Jenn: I am going to get right out there and say that if you don't have dark turkey or chicken meat to work with, you really need to substitute half the meat with beef or pork, or better yet, go to a different grocery store. Fat is the coin of the meatloaf realm, and you need a little bit of it from our feathered friends to make what will still be a less caloric loaf, in most cases, than its beef brethren. Having said that, we do not offer these meatloaves as alternatives to your Lean Cuisine. These are here because we find poultry an awesome vehicle for certain seasonings, and for heat, and we salute its ability, like a forty-year marriage, to hold together through all manner of trial.

Frank: What poultry does in a meatloaf that red meats don't is cede the stage somewhat. And that can be a good thing. A cook can work with that and profit from it. Poultry becomes the canvas—to switch metaphors—that lets the meatloaf's colors pop. In our Spicy Turkey Loaf with Sriracha (page 130), that Sriracha really registers. In our Buffalo-Style Chicken Loaf with Blue Cheese (page 119), the Buffalo sauce and cheese are especially bold. And of course the cheese in that loaf, combined with dark-meat chicken, helps ensure tenderness and even some gooeyness.

Jenn: Turkey, for its part, can also give a cheeky nod toward salad, as with our Charlie Bird Turkey Loaf with Farro (page 126), which combines the components of one of our favorite salads (the farro, the pistachio, the cheese) with the satisfying heft of a meat that doesn't run roughshod over greens and grains. Beef may have more atavistic zing, but poultry's blank stare allows the other flavors and textures to strut. A great example of this: Michael White's Chicken Eggplant Loaf (page 134), which has a fascinating interplay of eggplant and fennel. The former would get lost in a beef loaf. The latter, which nabs a Best Supporting Actress statuette in this loaf, would be unnoticed and unheralded: an extra listed in the credits with the stunt doubles.

Frank: Excuse me, *atavistic zing?* You, Jenn, have accused me in chapters past of not getting enough sleep; I hereby accuse you of spending too much time helping your older daughter study for vocabulary tests and the S.A.T. In regard to the Charlie Bird Turkey Loaf with Farro, we should point out that it's one of the healthiest loaves in the book; if a garden could grow a meatloaf, this is the meatloaf that the garden would grow. But I'm partial perhaps to the Buffalo-Style Chicken Loaf with Blue Cheese, because, like several other loaves in our book, it shows meatloaf's uncanny skills as an imposter, a facsimile, a mimic. It not only combines everything you'd find on a plate of chicken wings, down to the celery and carrot, but it also makes you believe, if you shut your eyes, that you're actually *eating* a Buffalo-style wing dipped (generously) in blue cheese.

Jenn: While we are sitting here getting all hot and bothered about poultry, let me add that it can carry the weight of the world. Or at least the flavors of the world. Let me opine if I may on the ecumenical vim—the planetary heterogeneity—of the turkey. (I think *some* of those words are S.A.T.-caliber, no?) Our Spicy Turkey Loaf with Sriracha is positively polyglot, though it favors the Asian tongues. You've got your soy, your cumin and of course your panko to plump it all up and fill in the cracks. It's not only very good; it's very easy. Like you.

Frank: You're confusing me with your muffins.

Jenn: So glad you brought those up. There is a whole underappreciated category of meatloaf *as* muffins, and they're a brilliant idea. The muffins can be a small meal that comes out of the oven already in individual portions, or they can be cocktail-party canapés or a first course. Turkey, for whatever reason, seems to be a great protein partner for the muffin tin, popping right out once cooked, which is what our Turkey Meatloaf Muffins (page 123) do. Further, unlike actual muffins, which involve leavening, meatloaf muffins don't rise and expand and spill out over the tin. They're tidy. We made these in a quasi-Italian style, with sundried tomatoes and lots of fresh herbs. If you're feeling all fancy, you could frost them, so to speak, with a mashed-potato hat.

Frank: A mashed-potato hat? I'm now picturing scalloped-potato scarves and baked-potato gloves. That's what we need in this world, every bit as much as poultry meatloaves: a winter wardrobe you can eat.

Buffalo-Style Chicken Loaf with Blue Cheese

Serves 6 to 8

Each chicken-lover has his or her favorite chicken part. We're all about the wing, with its optimal ratio of flavorful skin to meat. We're especially fond of the Buffalo-style chicken wing—so fiery, so tangy. And we were determined to reproduce its magic in a meatloaf.

The degree to which this meatloaf evokes the bar snack it mimics will amaze you. The celery and carrot sticks that often garnish Buffalo-style chicken wings are here, in different form. So is the blue cheese in which a Buffalo-style wing is often dipped. Be forewarned: If you're not a blue cheese–lover, this loaf isn't for you. If you are, grab a fork and dig in.

Making your own Buffalo sauce for the loaf is easier than you'd imagine and worth the minor effort for the vividness of its taste. To guarantee that this meatloaf isn't dry, use ground dark chicken meat, which may require a mail order or a visit to a butcher. We had good luck with kosher butchers.

There's heat in this dish, and if you're nervous about that, subtract one tablespoon of Tabasco, eliminate the cayenne pepper or do both. But first try it this way.

BUFFALO SAUCE

(about 1 cup)

8 tablespoons (1 stick) salted butter

½ cup Tabasco sauce or comparable Louisiana red hot sauce

1 heaping tablespoon tomato paste

1½ tablespoons white wine vinegar

½ teaspoon Worcestershire sauce

¼ teaspoon smoked paprika

¼ teaspoon cayenne pepper

LOAF

2 tablespoons salted butter

1 small white or yellow onion

½ cup finely chopped (or pulsed in a food processor) celery, no leaves (approximately 3 stalks)

⅔ cup finely chopped (or pulsed in a food processor) peeled carrots (packaged peeled baby carrots are fine)

2 cloves garlic, minced

2 pounds ground dark chicken meat

9 ounces medium-hard blue cheese such as Danish blue, crumbled with your fingers

½ teaspoon dried dill

½ teaspoon dried parsley

1 medium-sized egg, lightly beaten

½–1 cup unseasoned panko bread crumbs

FOR THE SAUCE

1. Melt the butter in a small saucepan over low heat. Add the rest of the sauce ingredients, raise the heat to medium and cook, whisking occasionally and watching closely. The minute the liquid begins to bubble, give it a final whisk, remove it from the heat and set it aside.

2. Now move on to making the loaf.

FOR THE LOAF

1. Preheat the oven to 350 degrees F. Line a 9-by-13-inch (or larger) glass or metal baking pan with nonstick aluminum foil.

2. In a large skillet over low heat, melt the butter. Add the onions, celery, carrots and garlic, stirring so they are thoroughly mixed. Increase the heat slightly and simmer for 10 to 12 minutes, stirring occasionally.

3. Transfer the vegetables to a large bowl and add the chicken, blue cheese, dill, parsley and egg. Whisk the Buffalo sauce anew so that it regains an even consistency, transfer it to a glass measuring cup and pour ⅔ cup of the sauce into the large bowl, holding the rest in reserve. Add ½ cup of the panko and mix everything together thoroughly with your hands, using kneading motions. It will have a loose consistency—this is the nature of ground dark-meat chicken, which hardens considerably in the cooking—but if it's so wet it clearly can't be shaped, add more panko, never exceeding 1 cup in all.

4. Transfer the mixture to the prepared baking pan, shaping it into a long loaf with a consistent width. Bake for 55 minutes, or until the internal temperature reaches 165 degrees F. Then remove the pan from the oven and let the loaf rest, uncovered, for at least 10 minutes.

5. After slicing the loaf into individual portions, whisk the remaining Buffalo sauce one more time, pour it into a tiny bowl or ramekin and with a spoon drizzle a very small amount of it over the slices for anyone who wants the extra heat.

Turkey Meatloaf Muffins

Serves 4 (makes 8 muffins)

Meatloaf batter has very little in common with cake batter, except for one salient and delightful quality: It can easily be poured into muffin tins, creating a neat and aesthetically pleasing take on the single serving (or half serving, in this case). This is a great recipe for a potluck because you can toss these gals onto a platter instead of turning out a loaf and getting stuck tableside cutting it into neat slices, which would prevent you from attacking the macaroni dish that always seems to go first.

Turkey is well suited to this recipe because it cooks a bit more quickly than beef, which was probably your goal for party portions. And the recipe gets a robust, distinctive Italian twist from the pairing of sun-dried tomatoes—which we think of as the Guns N' Roses of ingredients, very 1980s but still enjoyable in the right setting—with Parmesan, bread crumbs, basil and oregano.

LOAF

1 tablespoon olive oil, plus extra for greasing the tin

1 small onion, diced

1 medium carrot, peeled and grated

1 clove garlic, minced

2 teaspoons kosher salt

1 teaspoon freshly ground black pepper

1½ teaspoons Worcestershire sauce

1 pound ground dark turkey meat

1 cup unseasoned bread crumbs

2 eggs, lightly beaten

1 cup grated Parmigiano-Reggiano cheese

5 oil-packed sundried tomatoes, chopped

½ cup mixed fresh herbs (oregano, sage, basil and thyme leaves,
*   or a similar combination)*

GLAZE

4 oil-packed sundried tomatoes, chopped

¼ cup balsamic vinegar

¼ cup olive oil

1. Preheat the oven to 350 degrees F. Grease the cups of an 8-cup standard muffin tin with olive oil or, better yet, the oil from the jar of sundried tomatoes.

2. Heat the olive oil in a medium skillet over low to medium heat, add the onions and carrots and sauté until soft, about 10 minutes. Add the garlic. Stir in the salt, pepper and Worcestershire sauce. Cook until the garlic is soft, about another minute. Be careful not to burn the garlic.

3. Transfer the mixture to a large bowl. Add the turkey, bread crumbs, eggs, cheese, sundried tomatoes and herbs, and mix together with your clean hands until everything is just incorporated.

4. Put the glaze ingredients in a small bowl, and whisk until combined.

5. Divide the meatloaf muffin mixture into eight equal portions and pat them down into the prepared cups in the muffin tin, filling each cup only two-thirds of the way to the top.

6. Spoon the glaze on top of each muffin and spread it evenly.

7. Bake for about 25 minutes, or until a muffin's internal temperature reaches 165 degrees F.

8. Remove the muffins from the tins by running a knife along the inside of each cup if needed. Let them cool on a wire rack for 5 to 10 minutes before serving.

Charlie Bird Turkey Loaf with Farro

Serves 4

One of the best salads that we've tripped across in recent years is a mainstay at Charlie Bird, a favorite restaurant of ours in downtown Manhattan. It includes farro, mint, Parmesan and pistachios, so we decided to repurpose those ingredients and capture the flavors in a meatloaf.

Because this loaf is salad-inspired and because farro is such a nutritious alternative to bread crumbs, we kept the fat and calories in check by choosing ground turkey, though we do recommend dark-meat turkey for its extra juiciness. We added shiitake mushrooms, a terrific agent of "umami" that combines with the farro to bind the rest of the ingredients in a supple fashion. Green peas are here for their color as well as their taste. And we switched the Parmesan to pecorino, which is slightly more forceful. This all makes for a rich mix of tastes and textures.

Even so, this is among the subtler meatloaves in this book, so we've included a sweet glaze, which you can absolutely skip if you're making this for its healthful virtues.

LOAF

2 tablespoons olive oil

1 small onion, diced

3 cloves garlic, minced

½ pound (about 3½ cups) stemmed and roughly chopped fresh shii-
take mushrooms

1 cup cooked farro (see Note)

½ cup (densely packed) chopped fresh mint leaves

1⅓ cups grated pecorino cheese (grated on the large-hole side of
a box grater)

1 pound ground dark turkey meat

⅓ cup frozen peas, thawed

½ cup chopped shelled roasted pistachio nuts (you can buy them
this way)

1 large egg, lightly beaten

2 teaspoons salt

Freshly ground black pepper to taste

GLAZE

½ cup balsamic vinegar

⅔ cup honey

1 tablespoon grated lemon zest

1. Preheat the oven to 350 degrees F. Line a 9-by-13-inch (or larger) baking pan with parchment paper or aluminum foil; or use a large cast-iron skillet.

2. Warm 1 tablespoon of the olive oil in a small skillet over low heat, add the onions and sauté until almost soft, about 10 minutes. Add the garlic and cook for another 4 to 5 minutes. Remove from the heat and transfer to a large bowl to cool.

3. In the same skillet, add the remaining 1 tablespoon oil and the mushrooms and cook over low to medium heat until the mushrooms have shrunk and softened, 8 to 10 minutes.

4. Transfer the mushrooms to the bowl containing the onions and add all the remaining loaf ingredients; then mix together with your clean hands.

5. Form the mixture into a loaf in the prepared baking pan or the cast-iron skillet. Put it in the oven.

6. While the loaf begins cooking, combine the glaze ingredients in a small saucepan and cook over medium heat for about 20 minutes, stirring occasionally, until the mixture thickens to the consistency of syrup. Remove from the heat.

7. After the loaf has cooked for 20 minutes, spoon enough of the glaze over it to coat it entirely without drowning it—about half the glaze. There should be some left over.

8. Cook the loaf for another 20 minutes or until the internal temperature reaches 160 degrees F.

9. Remove the pan from the oven and let the loaf rest, uncovered, for 5 to 10 minutes; then slice it. Serve with the extra sauce on the side.

Note: Cook the farro according to the package directions in salted water, erring on the side of less time, not more. To get a yield of 1 cup, ½ to ²/₃ cup uncooked farro should do. Drain off the excess liquid before using.

One of the many virtues of our **Charlie Bird Turkey Loaf with Farro** is that it gets you halfway to Thanksgiving, and you can cover the rest of the distance as you transform it into a sandwich. Toast thick slices of a raisin-walnut bread or something like it and pair a cold or warmed slice of this loaf, or even half of one of the **Turkey Meatloaf Muffins** (page 123), with cranberries, cranberry jelly or a cranberry mayonnaise. Butter lettuce is the right roughage for this, and if you want to be ambitious, add a layer of roasted butternut squash to bring pumpkin into play. Channel the pilgrims. Enjoy.

Spicy Turkey Loaf with Sriracha

Serves 4

Wе will not apologize for the turkey.

Sure, this foolish fowl may make for bad burgers, and the sandwiches that we construct from them scream, "I'm in an interminable H.R. meeting and someone took the last roast beef on rye!" But ground dark turkey meat—and to be clear, that's all we are talking about here—makes for some mean meatballs, and when properly seasoned and gussied up, a mighty fine meatloaf, too. This one came to us from Erin McDowell, a food stylist and writer at Food52.com, the fabulous cooking website where a different version of the recipe was first published.

We tweaked, doing our onions and garlic in vegetable oil instead of sesame oil, though we enjoy that and you're welcome to try it, too. Instead of plain bread crumbs, we used panko, which works better.

You may wish to do an additional tweak of your own and double this, because it's great as a sack lunch, even served cold.

LOAF

1 tablespoon vegetable oil

1 medium yellow onion, diced

3 cloves garlic, minced

1 pound ground dark turkey meat

2 tablespoons spicy brown mustard

2 tablespoons tomato paste

3 tablespoons soy sauce

1 tablespoon rice vinegar

1 tablespoon Worcestershire sauce

2 teaspoons ground cumin

2 teaspoons ground coriander

1 teaspoon cayenne pepper, or more to taste

Salt and freshly ground black pepper to taste

1 large egg, lightly beaten

¾ cup unseasoned bread crumbs, preferably panko, or more as needed

SPICY SRIRACHA GLAZE

¼ cup ketchup

2 tablespoons apple cider vinegar

2 tablespoons Sriracha

1 teaspoon ground cumin

1. Preheat the oven to 350 degrees F. Line a rimmed baking sheet or a 9-by-13-inch (or larger) baking pan with parchment paper or aluminum foil.

2. Warm the oil in a medium-sized skillet over low to medium heat, add the onions and sauté until soft, about 7 minutes. Add the garlic and cook for 2 minutes more, taking care not to burn the onions. Transfer the onion mixture to a large bowl.

3. Add all the remaining loaf ingredients to the onion mixture, making sure they're fully integrated but not over-mixed. If the mixture feels too wet to be shaped, add more bread crumbs.

4. Transfer the mixture to the prepared baking sheet or pan and form it into a loaf with a consistent width.

5. In a small bowl, thoroughly combine all the ingredients for the glaze. Then brush the glaze generously over the top and sides of the loaf, holding enough glaze in reserve to baste the loaf occasionally during cooking.

6. Bake, basting occasionally with the glaze, until the loaf is cooked through, 35 to 45 minutes, or until the internal temperature reaches 165 degrees F. (If you like, you can run the finished loaf under the broiler to make the glaze form a bit of a crust.)

7. Remove the baking sheet from the oven. Let the loaf rest, uncovered, for 5 to 10 minutes, and then slice and serve.

Our **Spicy Turkey Loaf with Sriracha** has a whole lot going on, but one element it doesn't have is cheese. So introduce that as you turn it into a sandwich, and choose a *mild* cheese— provolone, Muenster, mozzarella—to tame the loaf's fire. Prepare the sandwich on a griddle or in a frying pan, using a lightly buttered, thick sourdough under the loaf and melting the cheese, grated, over it.

Serve open-faced.

Michael White's Chicken Eggplant Loaf

This recipe was conceived for us by the chef Michael White, who has restaurants around the world and a veritable Italian food empire in New York City, including Marea, on Central Park South, where finance-industry titans and show-business celebrities mingle. Needless to say, there's no meatloaf on its menu.

But there's meatloaf in Michael's soul.

This is it, and it's proof positive that white meat can travel far beyond its feathery flavor borders when it gets the right partners and seasoning. The fennel seed here gives that chicken a sausage-like quality. The eggplant contributes to a surprising texture and lends this loaf a pleasant earthiness. The cheese rounds it all out.

This recipe does have two baking steps, but they're both a cinch. First you cook the eggplant until it becomes crisp. You can be soaking your bread at the same time anyway. During a little visit with your blender, the eggplant is married to the bread to form a paste that incorporates beautifully with the ground chicken. The loaf pan helps it hold its structure, although you can cook it on a baking sheet, too. Be sure to watch it as it cooks: With ground poultry there's a fine line between undercooked and rubber.

Olive oil, for greasing the pan

1 large eggplant

2 slices white or whole-wheat
bread (crusts removed),
ripped into chunks

¼ cup heavy cream

2 pounds ground chicken,
preferably dark meat

2 teaspoons fennel seeds

2 cloves garlic, finely chopped

2 eggs, lightly beaten

1 cup panko bread crumbs

½ cup grated pecorino cheese

½ cup grated Parmigiano-
Reggiano cheese

1 tablespoon salt

1 cup roughly chopped fresh basil

1. Preheat the oven to 400 degrees F. Lightly grease a loaf pan with olive oil.

2. Slice the eggplant in half lengthwise, and then cut each half into quarters lengthwise. Place the eggplant pieces on a baking sheet and roast until softened, about 30 minutes. It will look a bit crispy. Worry not! Let it cool. Reduce the oven temperature to 350 degrees F.

3. While the eggplant is roasting, combine the bread with the heavy cream in a medium-sized bowl and soak for 15 minutes, until the liquid is absorbed.

4. Place the bread and the roasted eggplant into a blender and pulse until a paste is formed.

5. Combine the eggplant paste with all the remaining ingredients except the basil in a large standing mixer, and mix on low speed for about 1 minute, until fully incorporated. Then fold in the basil.

6. Press the meatloaf mixture into the prepared loaf pan and bake for about 1 hour, until the internal temperature is 165 degrees F.

7. Remove the pan from the oven and let the loaf rest, uncovered, for about 10 minutes before slicing and serving.

Hoisin Duck Loaf

Serves 6

In a way it's surprising that you don't run across more meatloaf recipes calling for duck, because it perfectly meets the criteria for meats best translated into loaves. It's fatty. It's flavorful. It can hold its own in the face of aggressive seasoning, and yet it has enough personality to carry the day without an array of co-conspirators and fanciful accents.

But ground duck is no cinch to find, and that explains its demure role in meatloaf cookery. For this recipe, you'll have to locate the right butcher and have a conversation with him or her, making clear that you want not just duck meat but duck skin and fat as well.

You'll be glad you did, because this dish is opulent, majestic. It's the Taj Mahal of poultry loaves, though that reference may not be exactly right, because China, not India, is the country summoned by the hoisin sauce and because this loaf is arguably ground meat's answer to Peking duck. We owe a special thanks to our food-writing friend Cathy Barrow, whose veggie loaf you'll find in a later chapter, for helping us develop this.

GLAZE

1 cup hoisin sauce

2 teaspoons Dijon mustard

1 teaspoon toasted sesame oil

1 teaspoon chopped fresh thyme

½ teaspoon grated orange zest

Pinch of freshly ground black pepper

LOAF

½ pound thick-cut smoked bacon, chopped

½ cup finely chopped shallots

½ cup sliced celery (½-inch-thick slices, cut on the diagonal)

½ cup slivered scallions (white parts)

2 eggs

¼ cup heavy cream

2 pounds ground duck including the skin and fat

   (generally 2 breasts will be enough)

¼ cup chopped dried tart cherries

2 tablespoons finely chopped fresh flat-leaf parsley

1½ teaspoons chopped fresh thyme

1 teaspoon grated fresh ginger

½ teaspoon grated orange zest

1½ teaspoons kosher salt

½ teaspoon freshly ground black pepper

1 cup fresh (soft) bread crumbs

2 tablespoons white sesame seeds, toasted (see page 230,

   Quick and Easy Super-Snappy Green Beans, for instructions)

1. To make the glaze, whisk together all of the glaze ingredients in a small bowl. Set it aside.

2. Preheat the oven to 375 degrees F. Line a rimmed baking sheet (with sides at least an inch high) with parchment paper.

3. In a medium-sized skillet, cook the bacon over medium heat until crisp. Remove the bacon with a slotted spoon and set it aside on paper towels to drain. Pour off all but 2 tablespoons of the bacon fat, add the shallots to the skillet and cook over low heat until translucent, 4 to 5 minutes. Add the celery and all but 1 tablespoon of the scallions. Stir to coat with the fat, and cook briefly, another 4 to 5 minutes. Remove from the heat and spread out on a plate to cool.

4. In a small bowl, whisk the eggs and cream together.

5. In a large bowl, combine the shallot and celery mixture, ground duck, cherries, parsley, thyme, ginger, orange zest, salt and pepper. Gently mix to combine, and then add the bread crumbs and the egg-and-cream mixture. Combine swiftly and with a light hand. Fold in the bacon pieces.

6. Form the duck mixture into a loaf on the prepared baking sheet and spoon the hoisin glaze generously over the surface of the loaf. Bake for 40 minutes, or until 155 degrees F in the center.

7. Remove the baking sheet from the oven, let the loaf rest slightly, uncovered, and then slide it onto a platter. Sprinkle the surface of the loaf with the toasted sesame seeds and the reserved tablespoon of scallions, and serve.

Jerk Chicken Loaf

We are not, for the most part, beach people. Perhaps because we eat significant quantities of meatloaf, we avoid parading around publicly in minimal clothing, lest we scare small children. So the Caribbean doesn't beckon us the way it does others.

But its flavors? Those we love, especially Jamaica's jerk chicken, which has currents of heat, wafts of sweetness and a sway and swagger all its own. It's the reggae of poultry, and this recipe captures that music.

We used habanero chiles because they're similar to Scotch bonnets (the true Jamaican ingredient) but much, much easier to find. And we've given you two options: a half-chicken, half-pork loaf, which is our stronger recommendation, or an all-chicken one, which won't be as moist but will bring the seasonings into sharper, edgier relief. If you go the all-chicken route, definitely use dark meat.

Finally, to tame the loaf's heat and bring more of the tropics into play, we recommend garnishing it with a fruit-based condiment.

1⅓ cups chicken stock or broth

2 tablespoons salted butter

2 teaspoons salt

1 cup uncooked long-grain white rice

1 shallot, minced

3 cloves garlic, minced

1 or 2 pounds ground dark (thigh) chicken meat

1 pound ground pork (if using only 1 pound ground chicken)

2 scallions (white and green parts), finely chopped

2 habanero chiles, stemmed, seeded and minced

2 heaping tablespoons dark brown sugar

2 teaspoons dried thyme

1½ teaspoons ground allspice

½ teaspoon Old Bay seasoning

½ teaspoon ground cinnamon

¼ teaspoon ground cloves

¼ teaspoon grated nutmeg

¼ teaspoon cayenne pepper

Grated zest from 1 lime

2 tablespoons fresh lime juice

1 tablespoon soy sauce

2 eggs, lightly beaten

1½ cups store-bought mango chutney, pineapple relish or
   sour cherry jam, for serving (optional)

1. Bring a combination of the chicken stock and ²/₃ cup of water to a boil in a saucepan, stirring in 1 tablespoon of the butter and 1 teaspoon of the salt. Add the rice and cook according to the rice package instructions. When the rice is done, remove the pan instantly from the

heat, fluff the rice and set it aside so it cools enough to be mixed by hand into the loaf.

2. Meantime, preheat the oven to 350 degrees F. Line a 9-by-13-inch (or larger) baking pan with nonstick aluminum foil or parchment paper.

3. Melt the remaining tablespoon of butter in a small saucepan. Add the shallots and cook over low to medium heat for about 5 minutes. Add the garlic and cook for another 3 to 4 minutes. Take off the heat and let cool slightly.

4. In a large mixing bowl, combine the ground meat, 2 tightly packed cups of the cooked rice, the remaining 1 teaspoon salt and the rest of the ingredients (except the chutney), mixing well with your clean hands. Transfer the mixture to the prepared baking pan and form it into a loaf. (Note: If you're using all chicken, its texture can be quite loose and watery, but so long as you can get it into a loaf shape, it will cook into a form that's firm enough to slice.)

5. Bake for 50 to 55 minutes, until a touch of the exterior determines it to be firm but not stiff, or until the internal temperature reaches 165 degrees F. Remove the baking pan from the oven and let the loaf rest for 5 to 10 minutes. Then slice it, edging each slice prettily with a few spoonfuls of your preferred chutney or relish, and serve.

FIVE

Meatless Loaves

Frank: OK, this is big fun. This is where we get to turn meatloaf on its head and challenge the basic assumption about it, which is that it's a thick, weighty mass of meat. It needn't be, not if you interpret meatloaf less literally and realize that it's merely the gelling, the joining, the thickening of a range of foods into one dish with room for them all. In that sense, it's salad made solid. But before we talk about some of the individual dishes in this chapter, Jenn, let's talk about our meaty ways: yours, mine, our country's, our world's. You're a pretty meaty lady, no?

Jenn: Indeed I am. Even meatless Mondays in my house sometimes involve a tad of bacon fat. Sue me. I have other weird culinary quirks that stem from a long tradition of meat-making in the home. I order salads out, and rarely assemble them myself, because I loathe all the chopping. When it comes to protein, I usually order fish in a restaurant, because that's something else that I make at home less often than I should. I figure I'll let the professional kitchen absorb the odor and figure out how to prevent skate from flipping up on its sad little wings. While I turn out a lovely halibut for a dinner party, and sauté kale with the rest of Americans in accordance with some sort of national decree, my weeknight rotation tends to involve chicken thighs, lollipops of lamb and the occasional steak. So I approached this chapter a tad apprehensive.

Frank: And I'm probably even meatier than you. I come from a family so beefy and porky that Mom kept an enormous extra freezer in the garage just for meat. And for much of my childhood, she had these meat services or meat plans (I can't remember precisely what they were called) deliver enormous orders of red meat—flank steaks, strip steaks, rump roasts, pork roasts, legs of lamb, racks of lamb and every iteration of bacon known to humankind—on a truck from Colorado, Oklahoma, Nebraska or some other livestock-friendly state. The truck came two or three times a year. As it disgorged its frozen bounty into our garage, my heart did a little jig. But with age I've grown fishier. (Fowler, too.) I've realized that there are times when my body and even my soul, if you'll forgive me, want a vacation from meat. So while I, too, approached this chapter with trepidation, I approached it with even more gratitude. And learned a lot along the way.

Jenn: The exploration of what vegetables and fish can do once bound together in the name of the loaf definitely became a fun culinary adventure and a bit of a food-science surprise. Eggs and binders are largely agnostic on their protein source: They'll date any of them, in the proper proportion. So here we bring on the beans, we tote the zucchini. And hello, sexy ahi.

Frank: "In the name of the loaf"—I like that. It gives meatloaf the religious aura it deserves. As for the seductions of ahi, fish actually makes more sense in a loaf than most people initially realize; you just have to think for a second about some of our usual uses for fish and how loaf-esque they already are. The fish terrine is really a fish loaf, or fishloaf, and that's illustrated by Melissa Clark's Salmon Loaf with Mustard and Capers (page 157). The crab cake is really a loaf in mid-aspiration, and we fulfill those ambitions with our Crab and Shrimp Loaf Muffins (page 161).

Jenn: What we also learned, and this was truly interesting, is that just as you can go high and low with meatloaf (ground beef to veal to lamb to the occasional bank-breaking cheese), so too can fish swim in shallow- and deep-pocketed waters. The Tuna Loaf Glazed with Mushrooms and Red Wine (page 153) is a special-guest extravaganza, perhaps, but let me speak in brief about the Tuna Melt Loaf (page 150), which is really just a few cans of tuna and beans dressed up in a pan, covered in cheese, and whipped together on a college kid's budget but with her mother's discretionary time. (Once those kids leave, moms tend to take up things like rowing and ill-advised attempts at writing a romance novel.) I especially love this loaf because it serves the exact same role as an actual tuna melt, providing precisely the comfort that I sought as a kid after soccer practice and that I still partake in now, midday, after someone at work has offered a few too many helpful hints.

Frank: I bet I could guess who those hint-givers are. But we won't bore our readers with *New York Times* gossip, and I can sense that you're itching to trade the sea for dry land and talk veggies.

Jenn: Yes. As we worked on this chapter, I was particularly interested to see where vegetarian-inclined cooks took the mandate of a vegetarian loaf. I speak of our dear friend Cathy Barrow, who is known as Mrs. Wheelbarrow to many who follow her tweets and recipes; she's a meat-lover with a vegetarian husband. And I refer to Daniel Patterson, whose San Francisco restaurant Coi specializes in turning veggies into prom queens.

Frank: Prom queens, let us add, who have a better night of things than Carrie did. Since you mention Cathy and Daniel and I just a bit ago mentioned Melissa Clark, I think this is the moment when we break into song, encouraging readers to sing along with us, and the music in this case is the Beatles, specifically "With a Little Help from My Friends." We got *a lot* of help from our friends, and it's our great fortune, and now our *readers'* great fortune, that our friends are so nimble in the kitchen.

Jenn: Yes. This entire book is like one long episode of *Barney & Friends*, without the creepiness. So go on.

Frank: The loaf that Cathy created for us, A Meatless Loaf for Dennis (page 172), shows that if you recruit the right players, your team can get into the playoffs and maybe even the Super Bowl without anything feathered, finned or hoofed. Meat needn't be the quarterback; it can sit on the bench. For example, Cathy uses pesto—with all its herbaceous, cheesy charms—in her loaf, and just as a bowl of linguini gets all the oomph it needs from basil and Parmesan, so does her loaf, though she then builds on them, going for broke with additional effects. By the time you've taken a few bites, meat's a distant memory, like the Bangles.

Jenn: I can't stress enough how much these loaves challenged my assumptions about texture and about flavor combinations. I confess I started out skeptical of the mixture of Parmesan and soy sauce in Daniel Patterson's Zucchini Loaf (page 164), but my doubts were forever lifted. It just works. I also underestimated the importance of following directions, ahem. While meat can be slapped around and manhandled with little ill effect, you really need to follow the directions for dicing, slicing or grating when it comes to your veggies. Failing to do so can have a sad impact on structure.

Frank: We should add that while the Tuna Melt Loaf and the Crab and Shrimp Loaf Muffins are fairly straightforward and easy, the rest of this chapter is for the slightly more patient, more meticulous cook. But if the cook's investment is greater with some of these recipes, so are the cook's rewards. You want to wow a dinner guest? Serve a meatless loaf that's as satisfying as a meaty one.

Jenn: Somehow this is all making me want to run to yoga. *Namaste.*

Tuna Melt Loaf

Serves 4

Among all the amazing meals we both have consumed across America's great cities, we might still choose a tuna melt as our last meal. Somewhat healthy—it's fish!—and deeply comforting in its lightly fried, cheesy goodness, the tuna melt is the ideal reward after swim practice, the best choice at the diner, the ultimate takeout lunch on a bad day at work. In this loaf, we have taken the tuna melt concept, given it a hint of spice and tucked it in a loaf pan for a fast weeknight dinner. It's comfort food, yes, but it's also protein-packed, getting an extra boost from the beans.

When you put this in the pan, it will somewhat resemble mush. But once baked, it's plenty firm and easily sliced. If you want some crunch, add some chopped celery. If you have guests—a crew team comes to mind—this can be doubled or even tripled and placed in a casserole dish, then sliced like cake. Another option: Pull it from the oven, take a fork and consume half of it alone while standing. You'll definitely be tempted.

1 teaspoon olive oil, plus extra for the pan

1 small red onion, finely chopped

1 7-ounce can tuna packed in olive oil (do not drain)

1 15-ounce can cannellini beans, drained and rinsed

3 tablespoons red wine vinegar

2 teaspoons fresh lemon juice

2 tablespoons fresh sage leaves, roughly chopped

1 teaspoon sea salt

¼ heaping teaspoon cayenne pepper

¼ teaspoon freshly ground black pepper

1 large egg, lightly beaten

1 cup panko bread crumbs

2 slices provolone cheese

1. Preheat the oven to 350 degrees F. Grease a loaf pan with olive oil.

2. Warm the 1 teaspoon olive oil in a small skillet over low to medium heat. Add the onion and sauté until soft, about 10 minutes.

3. In the meantime, use a large spoon to mix all the remaining ingredients except the provolone slices in a medium-sized bowl, mashing the beans a little with the back of the spoon as you mix.

4. Add the cooked onions and mix a bit more.

5. Plop the mixture into the prepared loaf pan, and place the slices of cheese on top of the loaf (they may overlap a bit). Bake for 30 minutes.

6. Remove the pan from the oven and let the loaf rest, uncovered, for about 5 minutes. Then slice and serve, or eat right from the loaf pan.

Tuna Loaf Glazed with Mushrooms and Red Wine

Serves 4

Mark Usewicz, the co-owner and fishmonger at Mermaid's Garden, a specialty fish market in Brooklyn, developed this loaf based on the store's tuna meatball. If you, like us, tend to think of ahi, which is the kind of tuna used in this loaf, as a just-for-sushi treat, this loaf is subversive—intentionally.

Mark is emphatic that good tuna does not need to be raw or quickly seared but is delicious if cooked with care. And this recipe is a reminder that high-quality protein elevates any loaf. It also underscores the versatility of tuna.

You're not limited to paying dearly for this dish, however. A lower-grade tuna—albacore, for example—will work, just not as impressively.

This dish takes longer than other loaves, for two reasons. One, the mixture needs to be made in advance and allowed time in the fridge for the bread crumbs to hydrate, a step that helps the loaf set. Two, there's a fair amount of chopping. Trust us: It's worth it.

While Mark calls the mushroom concoction in this recipe a glaze, that makes it sound dainty. It's not. It's a hearty topping—think somewhere between mashed potatoes and the famous French tomato "mother sauce"—that adds both succulence and flavor.

LOAF

2 tablespoons extra-virgin olive oil

½ cup diced onion

¼ cup diced fennel

¼ cup diced celery

1¼ pounds fresh tuna, preferably ahi, diced into ⅛-inch cubes

2 large eggs, lightly beaten

½ cup unseasoned bread crumbs

1 tablespoon kosher salt

1 teaspoon freshly ground black pepper

½ teaspoon smoked paprika

½ teaspoon ground sumac

2 tablespoons chopped fresh parsley

2 tablespoons chopped scallion greens

GLAZE

3 tablespoons extra-virgin olive oil

½ pound white mushrooms, sliced thin

Salt and freshly ground black pepper to taste

2 shallots, sliced thin

½ cup red wine

1 tablespoon red wine vinegar

1 bay leaf

1 clove

1 cup chopped fresh tomatoes

Pinch of red pepper flakes

½ teaspoon sugar

1. Line a baking sheet with parchment paper or aluminum foil.

2. Heat a heavy sauté pan over medium heat. Add the olive oil, onions, fennel and celery. Cook until softened but not browned, about 8 minutes. If the mixture begins to brown, add a splash of water to slow the cooking down. When the vegetables are soft, remove from the heat and allow the mixture to cool completely.

3. Place the cooled vegetables in a large mixing bowl. Add all of the other meatloaf ingredients and mix thoroughly with your clean hands. Place the bowl in the refrigerator and allow the mixture to chill for 30 minutes. During this time, preheat your oven to 425 degrees F and make the glaze.

4. To make the glaze, place the same heavy sauté pan, wiped clean with a paper towel, over high heat. Add 2 tablespoons of the olive oil to the pan, heat the oil and then add the mushrooms. Stir occasionally and cook until the mushrooms begin to brown. This will take 3 to 6 minutes depending on the strength of your burner. Season the mushrooms with salt and pepper, transfer them to a plate and set aside.

5. Place the same sauté pan over medium heat and add the remaining 1 tablespoon olive oil. Add the sliced shallots to the pan. After 30 seconds begin to stir the shallots, using your spoon to loosen any mushroom bits stuck to the pan. Cook the shallots until soft, about 2 minutes.

6. Add the red wine, vinegar, bay leaf and clove. Increase the heat to high and cook until the liquid has reduced by 90 percent.

7. When the liquid is reduced, add the tomatoes, red pepper flakes and sugar. Cook over medium heat until the glaze thickens, stirring occasionally to prevent it from scorching, about 20 minutes. The liquid should reduce by about half. Remove the pan from the heat, discard the bay leaf and clove and season the glaze with more salt and pepper. Fold in the cooked mushrooms and set aside.

8. Form the chilled mixture from the fridge into a rectangular loaf, about 2 inches high, on your prepared baking sheet. Bake for 15 minutes.

9. Remove the baking sheet from the oven and top the loaf with the tomato-mushroom glaze. Bake for another 15 to 25 minutes, until the internal temperature reaches 150 degrees F.

10. Remove the baking sheet from the oven and allow the loaf to rest, uncovered, for 15 minutes before slicing (use a serrated knife) and serving.

Melissa Clark's Salmon Loaf with Mustard and Capers

Serves 8

From the start of our meatloaf adventure, two of the elements that we knew we wanted in our book were these: a loaf that showcased salmon and a loaf devised by Melissa Clark, whose good kitchen sense and peerless kitchen skills are on weekly display in the *New York Times* and in her cookbook classics *Cook This Now* and *In the Kitchen with a Good Appetite*. This recipe is the confluence of those elements.

It's essentially a fish terrine, and it's a terrific digression from heartier, more gut-busting meatloaves. A word about its construction and cooking: You will pause and wonder about the volume of water in play. You will doubt. Don't, because the moisture is essential to proper results and because, as the recipe specifies, any excess liquid can easily be blotted up at the end. Blot with abandon. You're not rescuing a disaster. You're completing the intended paces and making sure this loaf turns out to be as supple as it should.

1½ tablespoons extra-virgin olive oil for skillet, plus 1½ teaspoons

for the loaf pan

1 onion, finely chopped

¾ pound boneless, skinless wild salmon fillet, cut into chunks

¾ pound boneless, skinless halibut, hake or other mild white fish
   fillet, cut into chunks

3 large eggs

½ cup panko bread crumbs

1 tablespoon Dijon mustard

½ teaspoon fresh lemon juice

2 teaspoons kosher salt

Pinch of freshly ground black pepper

1 large carrot, peeled and grated

1 teaspoon chopped fresh tarragon

1 tablespoon chopped capers

Boiling water for the water bath

1. Preheat the oven to 325 degrees F. Coat a 5-by-9-inch loaf pan with the 1½ teaspoons olive oil.

2. In a 10-inch skillet, heat the remaining 1½ tablespoons oil over medium heat. Cook the onions, stirring, until soft, 6 to 8 minutes. Set aside.

3. In a food processor, pulse the salmon and halibut until chopped but not pureed—you want texture here.

4. In a stand mixer, beat the eggs on medium speed until frothy, about 2 minutes. Beat in ¾ cup cold water and the onions, fish, panko, mustard, lemon juice, salt and pepper until well combined, about 2 minutes. Then beat in the carrots, tarragon and capers.

5. Transfer the mixture to the prepared loaf pan and smooth the top. Cover the pan with aluminum foil and transfer it to a large roasting

pan. Pour enough boiling water into the roasting pan to come halfway up the sides of the loaf pan. Bake until the terrine is firm in the center, 1 hour to 1 hour 20 minutes. Remove the loaf pan from the water bath, and let it cool for 10 minutes.

6. Blot any excess liquid from the top of the loaf with a paper towel. Run a butter knife around the edge of the pan to loosen the loaf. Invert a plate over the loaf pan, and holding the two together, flip the pan over. Tap the top and sides gently several times to help release the loaf onto the plate. Let it cool completely.

7. Soak up any more released juices with a paper towel. Slice and serve.

What do you do with a glistening slab of smoked or cured salmon? If you're a New Yorker or simply a sensible person, you put it on a bagel half that's been given a *schmear* of cream cheese, add a slice of tomato and maybe sprinkle a few capers on the affair. So follow that script with a cold leftover slice of **Melissa Clark's Salmon Loaf with Mustard and Capers**: Top it with a second bagel half or leave it open-faced; if the bagel's fresh, no need to toast it. An onion, plain, egg or everything bagel would be best.

Crab and Shrimp Loaf Muffins

Serves 4

(One muffin would be an adequate small appetizer.
Three would be a very generous entree.)

s we've noted before, the meatloaf has many culinary kinfolk: the meatball, the pâté, the hamburger. To this distinguished clan the crab cake can be added: It, too, involves a meat of sorts that's been stretched, and given shape, by the addition of binders.

Our crab and shrimp loaf muffins are in some ways crab cakes with more heft and with the ability to be molded into the taller, cuter form of muffins, which allows the use of a muffin tin in a cooking process that's especially easy and clean.

Think of the oyster crackers as bread crumbs that have had a brief beach vacation on Cape Cod. Be careful not to overcook the shrimp. And plan ahead, as the loaf batter needs time in the refrigerator so that the muffins are sure to hold together.

1 pound small shrimp, peeled and deveined

1 pound canned lump crabmeat (not jumbo lump)

1⅓ cups coarse oyster-cracker dust (created by smashing oyster crackers with your fingers or with a pestle; by placing them in

161

a large plastic bag and going over them with a rolling pin; or by

pulsing in a food processor. One large box of oyster crackers

will yield enough.)

5 tablespoons finely chopped fresh dill, plus a half dozen or so sprigs

for garnish

2 scallions (white parts), finely diced

½ cup mayonnaise

3 eggs, lightly beaten

1 heaping tablespoon Dijon mustard

1 teaspoon Old Bay seasoning

½ teaspoon cayenne pepper

¼–½ teaspoon salt, to taste

2 heaping teaspoons grated lemon zest

1 tablespoon fresh lemon juice, plus a half dozen or so lemon wedges

for garnish

1. Four to eight hours before mealtime, bring 1 quart of water to a boil in a large pot.

2. Place the shrimp in a steamer basket and set it in the pot (do not let the basket touch the water). Steam for just 3 to 7 minutes, until the shrimp barely begin to turn pink; do not cook through.

3. Transfer the shrimp to a large plate or medium-sized bowl and let them cool for 5 to 10 minutes. While they're cooling, drain and dry the crabmeat, making sure that any pieces of shell or cartilage are removed, and flake the meat with your fingers to break up any large lumps. Chop the cooled shrimp into small pieces.

4. Combine the shrimp, crabmeat and the rest of the ingredients (except the dill sprigs and lemon wedges) in a large bowl, mixing thoroughly with your clean hands. Cover the bowl with plastic wrap and chill in the refrigerator for 4 to 8 hours.

5. Preheat the oven to 375 degrees F. Spray a nonstick muffin tin with cooking spray.

6. Pack the crabmeat mixture tightly into the muffin cups, filling them to the top. The mixture should yield 8 to 10 muffins.

7. Bake for 18 to 21 minutes, until the muffins darken and harden enough to hold together. Remove the tin from the oven, let it cool for 3 to 5 minutes and then use a knife to gently separate the sides of the muffins from the cups and slide them out. Serve, garnishing each plate with a sprig of dill and a small wedge of lemon.

Daniel Patterson's Zucchini Loaf

This recipe was developed by Daniel Patterson, a chef who operates several successful restaurants in and around San Francisco, for a soup kitchen in Milan run by his friend Massimo Bottura. Called Refettorio Ambrosiano, the kitchen is a place where cooks are challenged to use whatever ingredients are available to make a beautiful meal.

Given old scraps of vegetables, a little bit of meat and lots of bread, Daniel invented what's basically an inverted loaf, with the vegetables and bread as the main ingredients rather than the binders, and the meat, which he had less of, as a sauce. (We don't include a meat sauce here, because this chapter is for people avoiding meat, but if you feel no need to do that, you can top the loaf with a favorite meat sauce of your own.) It's very important that you grate the squash as directed; on our first try, we were lazy and sliced it instead, and the structure was compromised. In fact, use a loaf pan to preserve the structure. In this case, it's your friend.

⅓ cup pearl barley

¾ cup lentils

2 tablespoons vegetable oil

½ cup finely chopped onion

1 tablespoon minced garlic

⅔ cup finely chopped mixed yellow and red bell peppers (while using both colors is ideal, all of one or the other is fine)

1¾ cups grated zucchini (grated on the large holes of a box grater, then squeezed to remove excess liquid)

¾ cup fresh shiitake mushrooms, stemmed and chopped into roughly ¼-inch pieces

¾ cup unseasoned bread crumbs

⅓ cup grated Parmigiano-Reggiano cheese

1 tablespoon red miso paste

2 teaspoons Asian chile sauce, such as Sriracha

1 teaspoon soy sauce

2 eggs, lightly beaten

Salt and freshly ground black pepper to taste

1. Bring a cup of water to a boil in a small saucepan, add the barley and cook until just tender, 35 minutes; then drain. At the same time, cook the lentils in a cup of boiling water in another small saucepan for 20 minutes, until just tender; then drain.

2. While the lentils and barley are cooking, heat the oil in a medium-sized sauté pan over medium heat. Add the onions and cook for 5 minutes, until they soften. Add the garlic and peppers and cook for 1 minute more. Remove from the heat and let cool to room temperature.

3. Preheat the oven to 400 degrees F.

4. In a large mixing bowl, combine the drained cooked grains with all the remaining ingredients; then add the cooled onion-pepper mix. Mix very well. The mixture should be moist but not overly wet. Taste

for seasoning, and add salt and pepper as necessary. If it's too dry, add another egg.

5. Spoon the mixture into a nonstick loaf pan and bake for 50 minutes or until the top of the loaf is brown and crisp. Let it cool to room temperature, about 20 minutes, which helps it to set up. Then slice the loaf with a bread knife. Alternatively, let it sit for only 15 minutes, accepting that it may crumble slightly—with no effect on its flavor—as you slice it.

Michael Schwartz's Kasha Loaf with Caramelized Onion Gravy

Serves 8

Let's say you fall in love with a vegetarian. We don't know how you, the owner of a meatloaf cookbook, allowed this to occur in your life. Perhaps it was her elegant *vinyasas* on the mat next to you at yoga class. Maybe it was his suave way of outsmarting a smarmy colleague you mutually dislike. Whatever the case, you want to impress your vegetarian, so you make this loaf. It's a hearty, complex and deeply original recipe from the Miami chef Michael Schwartz, and it reflects his special regard for vegetables and grains, along with his genius for sensing the dazzling potential of ingredients that other cooks overlook.

It's time-consuming, and chances are you'll need to go shopping. Unlike most loaves in this book, this one has to be made in a nonstick loaf pan, which is nice to have around anyway, as it's ideal for banana bread. And it's more important with this loaf than with others not to substitute ingredients; doing so could ruin the structure.

As soon as you pull this from the oven, you will be entranced with the evocative kasha aromas. And each bite of it emphasizes a different ingredient—hello, spinach; nice to see you, ricotta—though those ingredients combine gorgeously as a whole.

3 cups vegetable stock

6 tablespoons (¾ stick) unsalted butter

1½ teaspoons sea salt, plus more to taste

½ teaspoon freshly cracked black pepper, plus more to taste

4 large eggs

1½ cups kasha (coarse granulation, which is important)

3 tablespoons extra-virgin olive oil

4 cups minced white onions

1 pound cremini mushrooms, washed, stemmed,
    caps pulsed 10 times in a food processor

4 cloves garlic, minced

1 tablespoon tomato paste

1 teaspoon fresh thyme leaves

2 tablespoons Worcestershire sauce

2 tablespoons soy sauce

1 pound spinach, blanched, cooled, squeezed and finely chopped
    (you may substitute frozen, thawed and well squeezed)

¾ cup ricotta cheese

¾ cup grated Parmigiano-Reggiano cheese

Caramelized Onion Gravy (recipe follows)

1. Preheat the oven to 375 degrees F.

2. To prepare the kasha, start by combining the vegetable stock, 3 tablespoons of the butter, 1 teaspoon of the salt and ¼ teaspoon of the pepper in a pot and bring it to a boil.

3. Meanwhile, lightly beat one of the eggs and add it to the kasha in a

medium-sized bowl, stirring to coat the kernels. In a large skillet over high heat, toast the egg-coated kasha, stirring often, for 2 to 3 minutes. Pour in the boiling stock and reduce the heat to low. Stir the kasha and cover the skillet. Cook for 8 to 10 minutes, until all the liquid has been absorbed and the kasha is tender. Turn off the heat and let it sit for 10 minutes, covered, and then transfer it to a large mixing bowl and set it aside to cool.

4. To make the loaf, place a large skillet over medium heat and add the olive oil and the remaining 3 tablespoons of butter. When the butter has melted, add the onions and season with ½ teaspoon of the salt and ¼ teaspoon of the pepper. Cook, stirring occasionally, until the onions are a deep golden brown and caramelized, roughly 20 minutes.

5. Add the mushrooms and garlic to the onions and sauté for 5 to 7 minutes, stirring regularly. Add the tomato paste, thyme, Worcestershire and soy sauce and simmer for 2 to 3 minutes. Remove from the heat. When the mixture has cooled slightly, add it to the kasha along with spinach, ricotta and Parmesan. Lightly beat the remaining 3 eggs and add them to the bowl. Mix thoroughly and adjust for seasoning.

6. Transfer the mixture to a nonstick loaf pan and pack it down with a spatula and by lightly tapping the pan on the table. Bake for 1 hour, until the loaf is brown on top and the edges are starting to pull away from the pan. Remove the pan from the oven and let the loaf rest for 10 to 15 minutes before sliding it out of the pan. Slice, and serve with Caramelized Onion Gravy. The gravy gives this loaf a very smothered-in-a-good-hot-mess-feel. The gravy may be made ahead or omitted, since the loaf is delicious without it, too.

Caramelized Onion Gravy

Makes 3 cups

2 tablespoons olive oil

2 tablespoons butter

3 cups minced onions

½ teaspoon kosher salt

½ teaspoon freshly cracked black pepper

2 tablespoons all-purpose flour

2 cups vegetable stock

1. Place a large skillet over medium heat and add the oil and butter.

2. When the butter has melted, add the onions and season with the salt and pepper. Cook, stirring occasionally, until the onions are a deep golden brown and caramelized, roughly 20 minutes.

3. Add the flour and stir for 1 minute. Add the stock and simmer for 2 to 3 minutes.

4. Puree the mixture in a blender or food processor, and season to taste.

A Meatless Loaf for Dennis

Our friend Cathy Barrow once conducted a contest concerning charcuterie. She was a fishmonger. She wrote a cookbook devoted in part to home-curing, -smoking and -brining meats and fish.

But all of that was useless to her husband, Dennis, who's a vegetarian. So meat-free options like this loaf make a regular appearance on her table. The key to this loaf, which has an amazing lasagna-like texture, is the delicious borlotti beans (Cathy, of course, cans her own). If you can't find any, use cannellini beans for a similar result. This loaf doesn't take long to cook, but if the top starts to darken too much before it's done, consider putting foil over it for the last 15 minutes of cooking. Don't be nervous: This loaf naturally has a dark color.

Like all veggie loaves, it's cooked in a loaf pan to assist with its structure. You use any other kind of pan at your risk, against our advice, and to our considerable disappointment.

LOAF

Grapeseed oil or nonstick cooking spray, for the loaf pan

1 cup unseasoned bread crumbs

¼ cup whole milk

2 tablespoons olive oil

1 small onion, diced

2 cloves garlic, minced

4 sundried tomatoes packed in oil, diced, oil reserved

1 carrot, peeled and finely diced

10 ounces frozen spinach, thawed and all moisture squeezed out

Kosher salt and freshly ground black pepper to taste

2 14-ounce cans borlotti or cannellini beans, drained and rinsed

½ cup fresh ricotta cheese

½ cup grated pecorino cheese

½ cup store-bought basil pesto (or your favorite recipe, if you are like Cathy)

TOPPING

⅓ cup tomato paste

2 tablespoons oil from the sundried tomatoes

1. Preheat the oven to 350 degrees F. Lightly oil or spray a 9-by-4-inch loaf pan.

2. In a small bowl, combine the bread crumbs and milk and set them aside.

3. In a large skillet, heat the olive oil over medium heat until shimmering. Add the onions and cook until they are translucent, about 8 minutes. Then add the garlic and continue cooking for a minute or two, taking care not to burn anything.

4. Stir in the sundried tomatoes, carrots and spinach and cook until the carrots are tender, about 5 minutes. Remove the pan from the heat. Season with salt and pepper.

5. Add the beans to the pan (still off the heat), stir and then add the bread crumb mixture, ricotta, pecorino and pesto and stir well but gently so the beans retain their shape. Taste the mixture and adjust the salt and pepper, if necessary.

6. Fill the loaf pan with the mixture and then knock the pan on the counter a few times to settle the mixture and eliminate any air pockets.

7. In a small bowl, stir together the tomato paste and oil for the topping, and then slather that over the loaf.

8. Bake in the center of the oven for about 50 minutes until it appears firm. Remove the pan from the oven and let the loaf rest, uncovered, for 10 minutes before slicing and serving.

Your meatloaf's second act needn't come between two slices of bread. Why not repurpose it as a pizza? That's the perfect reincarnation of **A Meatless Loaf for Dennis,** whose combination of cheeses (pecorino, ricotta) and flourishes (sundried tomatoes, pesto) already sound like the toppings of an inventive pizza. Use your favorite flatbread or even an uncut pita round, gloss it with some olive oil, crumble leftover loaf on the surface and heat in the oven or toaster oven at 350 degrees until warm, about five to seven minutes. To guard against dryness, perhaps grate a bit more pecorino over the top of the pizza before it goes into the oven.

∾ SIX ∾

Guilty Pleasures

Jenn: Meatloaf is, by its very nature, a guilty pleasure. It embraces fat. It asks to be bathed in things salty, sweet, spicy and caloric. But in this chapter we up the ante even further, tossing in elements that raise the guilt level several rosary beads. Cheese does not merely grin in some of these loaves; it cackles. Meat meets more meat. Binders are plucked from their own shelf of guilt and join the meatloaf party, which in this chapter is more like an orgy.

Frank: This may well be our cheesiest chapter. I always say that on the journey to meatloaf, there's a fork in the road, with cheese in one direction and no cheese in the other. That's your basic crossroads. That's your decision point. I prefer to turn the wheel toward Cheddar, toward Danish blue, toward ricotta. And I don't consider that an excursion in guilt. More like an exercise in living—and in doing right by meatloaf, which deserves a fate that's gooey, not dry. Cheese delivers that destiny.

Jenn: Indeed, *every* meatloaf in this chapter brings cheese into play, from provolone to your beloved blue, from a radical reimagining of the cheeseburger (page 180) to a meaty tribute to the taco (page 183).

Cheese brings a richness and fulsomeness to these loaves while also providing some of the salty kick that enhances the rest of the flavors and the whole experience. What's interesting is that most classic loaves do not in fact involve cheese, so we may have actually reinvented the wheel here. But I'd like to move on to bread crumbs.

Frank: We should, so we can discuss how far meatloaf can travel from bread crumbs. And this chapter is distinguished by the distance of that trip. Please fill readers in.

Jenn: Readers, you are now seniors in the Meatloaf Academy, poised for graduation, so you well know that eggs and some form of a crumb are the workhorses of meatloaf, bringing everything else together. In this chapter we show how liberal the interpretation of "some form of crumb" can be, and we perfect the pairing of unexpected carbs and the central, showcased protein. In the Frito Pie Loaf (page 195), for example, that carb is crushed Fritos, and you'll be wowed by the delicious Frito-ness of the resulting dish. Because a cheeseburger should be consumed with chips or fries, we put those chips right into the Cheeseburger and Fries Loaf (page 180).

Frank: I think of this not only as our cheesy chapter but also as our chippy chapter. Or would that be our chipper chapter? The chips, be they potato, corn or tortilla, actually make great sense, and they illustrate as well as any meatloaf ingredient the way a loaf combines a meal's protein and its starch—and even, sometimes, its vegetable or vegetables—into one multifaceted dish that's an impressively efficient nutrition delivery system. Our Mashed Potato Meatloaf (page 201) is the wedding of the entree and the side in one seriously filling loaf.

Jenn: For so many of us growing up, meatloaf on the plate signaled that mashed potatoes would be nearby. At some point, someone in the world decided that it was a crime to divorce that which should be lawfully wedded, and came up with the idea of having the cow and the spud tie the knot in one loaf. We take things further, letting the beef and potato honeymoon with cheese: in this case, a bit of Parmesan. I guess the honeymoon is in Italy, which is in line with another of this chapter's themes, our love of all things Italian.

Frank: *All Things Italian:* That could be the title of my memoir. Or a sign above my pantry. Or an OkCupid wish list. I want to pick up, though, on something else that you said sometime back in the other lands of loaves: "surprise." Meatloaf is often about surprise, and the recipes in this chapter are cases in point. There's a Russian-doll quality to them, with something concealed within, waiting to be discovered: the ham in the Volpe Family Loaf (page 190), the spiraled layer of carrots, spinach and prosciutto in Mario Batali's Stuffed Meatloaf (page 186).

Jenn: The Batali kitchen and the Volpe family offer us high and low versions of another loaf tradition: meat in meat. Ham has long served as a rejoinder to beef in the loaf, paired with some form of sliced cheese and rolled like a *bûche de Noël.* It's a fabulous family dish, meant to stretch each form of protein and to provide something festive and easily made on a Sunday night. Mario Batali takes mom's loaf and puts it in a Badgley Mischka gown, with a more sophisticated (and, yes, pricier) cheese and pork combination. Because he's a chef, it's more work, too. We love both loaves—one to eat in front of the football game, the other to serve to guests.

Frank: For a second or two, I didn't register all the words in one of your sentences and it became "Mario Batali in a Badgley Mischka gown." And I thought, wow, we really need to provide readers with a picture of that.

Jenn: Preferably with those orange clogs of his.

Cheeseburger and Fries Loaf

Serves 6

The kinship of the meatloaf and the hamburger gave rise to an obsession: We were determined to develop a meatloaf that closely approximated a cheeseburger not just in its taste but in its ingredients, relying on deconstructed burger elements and the most common burger condiments. To that end we banished Worcestershire and leaned instead on ketchup, mustard and mayonnaise.

We exiled onions, which are such signifiers of classic meatloaf.

To summon a sesame-seed bun, we included some toasted sesame oil. One version that we tried as we developed this used torn bits of actual buns in place of bread crumbs, but this final recipe goes in a slightly different direction, using potato chips to bring a bit of French-fry flavor into the equation. Use baked potato chips, so that there isn't too much oil released into the loaf, and if you like the way this turns out and want to experiment in the future, you can try flavored baked potato chips of your liking.

You've probably figured out that this isn't among the healthier meatloaves in the world—or in this book. But it's satisfying and *very* easy to make, and it's kid-friendlier than meatloaves with onion or potent spices. It's a cheeseburger writ large, a cheeseburger in extremis. A cheeseburger, that is, with fries baked right into it.

1½ cups crushed baked potato chips (1 large, not individual-sized,

bag of chips will yield enough; see Note)

1½ cups tightly packed shredded sharp Cheddar cheese

2 pounds ground chuck

2 eggs, lightly beaten

⅔ cup ketchup

2 heaping tablespoons Dijon mustard

⅓ cup mayonnaise

1 heaping tablespoon tomato paste

1½ teaspoons toasted sesame oil

1. Preheat the oven to 350 degrees F. Line a rectangular glass or metal baking pan (at least 9 by 13 inches) with nonstick aluminum foil.

2. In a large bowl, using your hands in kneading motions, mix together the crushed chips, the beef, the cheese, the eggs, ⅓ cup of the ketchup, 1 heaping tablespoon of the mustard and all of the mayonnaise.

3. Transfer the mixture to the prepared baking pan and shape it into a loaf whose width is consistent except at the slightly tapered ends. Put the pan in the oven.

4. While the loaf begins baking, put the remaining ⅓ cup ketchup, the remaining 1 heaping tablespoon mustard, the tomato paste and the

sesame oil in a small bowl, and, using a fork, whisk together until fully blended into a glaze.

5. When the loaf has been cooking for about 20 minutes, slide it from the oven for a few seconds—just long enough to use the back of a spoon or a rubber spatula to coat the top of the loaf with half of the glaze. Bake for another 20 minutes, and then use the remainder of the glaze to refresh the top of the loaf and to coat the upper halves of the sides. Continue to bake the loaf for another 15 minutes, or until the internal temperature has reached 145 degrees F for medium-rare.

6. Remove the loaf from the oven and let it rest, uncovered, for 10 minutes; then slice and serve.

Note: To crush the potato chips, put them in a medium-sized bowl and use your fingers to turn them into fine bits but not all the way into dust. They should look more like rice than like sand.

Just because something's obvious doesn't mean it's wrong. What you should do with a cold or warmed slice of the **Cheeseburger and Fries Loaf** is... make a cheeseburger! You're not just bringing it full circle, you're seizing a chance to lighten its heaviness with a beef patty's classic accessories: a thick slice of tomato, lettuce (preferably Romaine or Boston), pickles and a toasted bun. We recommend a robust deli mustard rather than ketchup, though the latter also works.

Taco Meatloaf

Serves 6

The meatloaf is the *Talented Mr. Ripley* of entrees, inasmuch as it can appropriate another food's personality and do an utterly persuasive, charismatic imitation. This one is a perfect example. Eating it, you'll experience a moment of happy disorientation because your palate and brain will be saying "taco" while your eyes are saying "meatloaf."

Our taco meatloaf has the additional virtue of being a vacation from the chop-chop-chopping of many other loaves because the store-bought salsa includes many of the ingredients that would otherwise necessitate knife work. The recipe works best if you use fresh salsa rather than jarred, which would have more liquid and less nuance. But store-bought packaged mixes of shredded cheese—Kraft's "Mexican Taco" blend, for example—do work well and are perfectly fine to use; the most important aspect of the cheeses in this recipe is that they're consistent with what you'd sprinkle into a hard-shell taco.

1½ cups crushed tortilla chips (1 large bag will yield enough; see

   Notes)

2 pounds ground chuck or other ground beef that's not too lean

½ cup mixed shredded Cheddar and
    Monterey Jack cheeses or store-
    bought taco blend

½ cup sour cream

1 cup your favorite hot salsa,
    preferably fresh

2 eggs, lightly beaten

1 tablespoon chili powder

2 teaspoons ground cumin

2 teaspoons salt

½ teaspoon red pepper flakes

½ teaspoon dried oregano

½ teaspoon hot (not smoked) paprika

½ teaspoon freshly ground black
    pepper

3–4 slices sharp Cheddar cheese

1. Preheat the oven to 350 degrees F. Line a 9-by-13-inch (or larger) glass or metal baking pan with nonstick aluminum foil. (This meatloaf is also a good candidate to make in a large cast-iron skillet.)

2. Place the crushed tortilla chips in a large bowl, and add all the remaining ingredients except the slices of cheese. Mix together by kneading with your clean hands, blending thoroughly but stopping once everything is incorporated. Transfer the mixture to the prepared baking pan and shape it into a loaf, taking care to keep the width consistent except for the tapering at the very ends.

3. Bake for 45 minutes, or until the internal temperature reaches 145 degrees F for medium-rare. Then slide the pan out of the oven just long enough to drape the slices of cheese over the top of the loaf so that they cover its length and overlap only slightly. Bake for another 5 to 10 minutes, until the cheese is melted but isn't sliding off the loaf. Remove the loaf from the oven and let it sit for 10 minutes, uncovered, before slicing.

Notes: To crush the tortilla chips, toss them into a large bowl and get your fingers working, turning the chips into small bits but not into dust. Alternatively, use the food processor, but pulse carefully—again, so you don't wind up with dust.

If you have leftover salsa and sour cream, you can put them on the table as additional condiments. You can also garnish each serving of meatloaf with a wedge of ripe avocado.

tomorrow's
LUNCH

Our **Taco Meatloaf** doesn't include avocado, which is waiting to claim its place in a sandwich the next day. Lightly toast 2 thick slices of sourdough. Mash one half of a super-ripe Hass avocado and spread it on one of the slices. Sprinkle some sea salt on the avocado; then add leftover loaf, diced tomato and a spritz of lime juice. This production is ideally rounded out with some fresh cilantro leaves and *queso fresco* if you have either or both on hand.

Mario Batali's Stuffed Meatloaf

Serves 6 generously

Mario Batali needs no introduction, and his recipe for meatloaf is exactly what you might expect—richly flavored, intensely meaty, Italian-leaning and requiring a bit of skill and patience.

This is in some sense a classic rolled loaf, with meat encasing meat, swimming in juices emanating from meat. Unlike many meatloaves, which are inherently budget-friendly, this one uses high-quality ingredients that greatly increase its expense. You want to buy good cheese, a caciocavallo if possible, and you want really nice prosciutto. The rolling of the meat is exciting and fun; just be sure you make it good and tight so it does not spread too much as it cooks. The pan juices make for a lovely, if slightly odd-colored, gravy. Embrace the difference!

This is a very rich loaf, and you will want a nice big salad or vegetable side to go with it. Then, a nap.

2 large carrots, peeled and cut into narrow strips about 12 inches long

1 pound lean ground beef

1 pound ground pork

1½ cups fresh bread crumbs

MARIO BATALI'S stuffed meatloaf

— cheese
— prosciutto
— carrots
— spinach
— meat
— bread crumbs

1 cup freshly grated pecorino cheese (about 3 ounces)

3 large eggs, lightly beaten

1 teaspoon kosher salt, plus more to taste

½ teaspoon freshly ground black pepper plus more to taste

1½ tablespoons all-purpose flour

2 cups frozen spinach, thawed, squeezed dry and chopped

6 thin slices prosciutto (about 4 ounces)

¼ pound sliced caciocavallo or provolone cheese

2 tablespoons extra-virgin olive oil

2 sprigs fresh rosemary

1 cup dry red wine

1. Preheat the oven to 400 degrees F.

2. Fill a medium-sized saucepan with salted water and bring it to a boil over high heat. Add the carrots and cook until tender, about 7 minutes. Using a slotted spoon, transfer the carrots to a plate.

3. In a large bowl, combine the beef with the pork, 1 cup of the bread crumbs, the pecorino, the eggs, 1 teaspoon salt and ½ teaspoon pepper; mix well with your clean hands.

4. Line a work surface with a 15-inch-long sheet of plastic wrap. In a bowl, mix the flour with the remaining ½ cup bread crumbs. Sprinkle the crumb mixture all over the plastic wrap. Transfer the meatloaf mixture to the crumb-lined plastic wrap, and press it into a 12-by-10-inch rectangle, about ½ inch thick. Lay the spinach over the meat, making sure it is evenly distributed, leaving a 1-inch border on the short sides.

5. Arrange the carrots over the spinach, and top with the prosciutto and sliced cheese. Starting from the long end of the plastic wrap closest to you, tightly roll up the meatloaf, tucking in the filling and using the plastic wrap to guide you; then discard the plastic wrap. Drizzle the meat loaf with the olive oil.

6. Put the rosemary sprigs in the bottom of a broiler pan and pour in the red wine. Cover with the broiler pan grate. Set the meatloaf on top of the grate. Bake for 35 minutes. Then turn the pan around and pour ½ cup of water through the grate. Continue baking for about 20 minutes longer, until an instant-read thermometer inserted in the center of the loaf registers 165 degrees F. Remove the pan and let the loaf rest, uncovered, for 10 minutes.

7. Discard any cheese from the bottom of the pan and strain the pan juices into a small saucepan. Boil the pan juices over high heat until

reduced to 1 cup, about 5 minutes. Pour into a serving bowl and season with salt and pepper.

8. Using a serrated knife, slice the loaf into 1-inch-thick slices and serve, passing the pan juices at the table.

Volpe Family Loaf with Ham

Serves 8

Our colleague Paul Volpe has strong memories of the meatloaf made by his family in western New York, a loaf that combines the traditional elements of beef and pork spiked with tomato juice—generally V8—and Italian seasonings with the fatty fun of ham hidden inside. The results were so good, they often had to employ the Volpe FHB, or family-hold-back rule, which dictates that guests eat first, just to make sure there is enough. What's nice about this recipe is that you can take it a few different ways, depending on your budget, and it will still seem fancy.

You can get any old ham at the grocery store of course, as long as it is thinly sliced, but if you get the really nice Italian-style ham sold at the meat counter, so much the better. Ditto for the mozzarella cheese; the cheap stuff is fine—this is meatloaf, not a cheese course—but if you get good fresh mozzarella, it will give your loaf a nicer dairy tang. We definitely recommend a cast-iron pan for this, because the loaf produces a lot of drippings that might well get crusty on a baking pan but collect into a perfect gooey sauce in said pan.

LOAF

1 pound ground beef

1 pound ground pork

2 small onions, finely chopped

2 eggs, lightly beaten

1 cup fresh bread crumbs

1 cup tomato juice, V8 juice, or plain tomato sauce

1½ teaspoons dried oregano

1 teaspoon dried thyme

½ cup fresh basil leaves, roughly chopped

½ teaspoon salt

¼ teaspoon freshly ground black pepper

8 slices any style ham, sliced thin by the gentleman (or lady) at
    the meat counter (preferably)

½ pound grated mozzarella

GLAZE

1 cup tomato sauce

1 tablespoon brown sugar

2 tablespoons red wine vinegar

1. Preheat the oven to 350 degrees F.

2. In a large bowl, use your clean hands to combine all the loaf ingredients except the ham and cheese.

3. Place the meatloaf mixture on a large piece of plastic wrap, and form it into a wide log.

4. Arrange the ham slices evenly on top of the log, and sprinkle with the cheese.

5. Starting from the long end of the plastic wrap closest to you, tightly roll up the meatloaf, tucking in the filling and using the plastic wrap to guide you; then discard the plastic wrap.

6. Place the loaf in the center of a cast-iron pan and pat the seams closed. Bake for 20 minutes.

7. In the meantime, combine the glaze ingredients in a small saucepan and cook over low heat until the brown sugar has dissolved.

8. When the loaf has cooked for 20 minutes, slather it with the glaze and continue to cook for roughly 40 more minutes, until the internal temperature reaches 155 degrees F.

9. Remove the pan from the oven and let the loaf rest, uncovered, for 10 minutes before slicing. Spoon the pan sauce over the slices.

Homely Homey Blue and Bacon Loaf

Serves 4 to 6

I f you can't tell a book by its cover, then you can't tell a meatloaf by its color. This one, we admit, has a faintly gray hue. There's no getting around that.

But there's ample reason not to care, because what it lacks in beauty it makes up for in deliciousness. This meatloaf is an off-the-charts indulgence for anyone who loves blue cheese and especially for anyone whose idea of the perfect cheeseburger is one topped with blue cheese and then a few slices of bacon to boot.

You want to pay attention to the quality of that blue cheese, and you want to make sure it's a hard enough blue cheese to crumble and mix with the other ingredients. You also want to use a baking dish that's big enough for ample room around the loaf because this loaf releases quite a bit of liquid during the cooking.

8–10 slices of your favorite bacon

1 small onion, diced

1½ pounds ground beef (chuck or sirloin so long as it's not too lean)

9 ounces blue cheese (Danish blue is preferable), crumbled

⅓ cup sour cream

1 cup unseasoned bread crumbs

2 eggs, lightly beaten

1 tablespoon Worcestershire sauce

1½ tablespoons Dijon mustard

1 teaspoon salt

1 teaspoon freshly ground black pepper

1. Preheat the oven to 350 degrees F. Line a 9-by-13-inch (or larger) baking dish with nonstick aluminum foil.

2. In a large skillet, fry the bacon slices, a few at a time, over medium heat until quite crisp; then remove and let drain on paper towels, leaving the fat in the skillet.

3. Add the onions to the bacon fat in the skillet and cook over low to medium heat for 10 to 12 minutes, until soft and somewhat translucent. With a slotted spoon, so as not to capture too much fat, transfer the onions to a large bowl. Crumble the bacon slices (patted dry with paper towels) into that bowl. Add the rest of the ingredients and mix thoroughly with your clean hands until all the ingredients are combined.

4. Transfer the mixture to the prepared baking dish and shape it into a loaf whose width is consistent except at the slightly tapered ends. Bake for 55 minutes, or until the internal temperature reaches 145 degrees F for medium-rare.

5. Remove the pan from the oven and let the loaf rest, uncovered, for 10 minutes before slicing. Spoon the excess juices from the baking dish over the slices if you want to be off-the-charts hedonistic.

Frito Pie Loaf

Serves 6

Texas offers us many culinary pleasures, from an array of regional barbecue styles to fajitas to pho to increasingly inventive new American cuisine in the state's big cities. But one of our favorites has always been the Frito Pie. Consumed at Little League games, at rodeos, at picnics and in living rooms, Frito Pie just might be the national dish of the Lone Star State, if it were indeed its own nation, which it once was and many residents of course believe it should be.

Frito Pie's ingredients begin with a pair of scissors, used to cut open an individual bag of Fritos, the corn chip that needs no further introduction. Then you dump a big old spoonful of chili into the bag. Grab fork. Consume. Preferably with a beer, or a Dr Pepper.

For this dish, inspired by Frito Pie, we take some of the essentials of Texas chili—Ro-Tel tomatoes, beef and cumin—and reconstruct it into one simple loaf. Texans would sniff at our addition of kidney beans (you may use pinto if you prefer) because Texas chili does not accommodate legumes. But we found the beans helpful for the loaf's structure and its texture. Some exciting additions could include a dollop of sour cream, some sliced Hass avocados or just more cheese. Who ever objected to more cheese?

1 tablespoon neutral oil, such as vegetable or grapeseed,

    plus extra for the loaf pan

1 small onion, diced

3 cloves garlic, minced

1½ pounds ground chuck

2 cups crushed Fritos (crushed into small pieces with your hands)

1 14-ounce can kidney beans, drained and rinsed

1 10-ounce can Ro-Tel Diced Tomatoes & Green Chilies, drained

1 large egg, lightly beaten

1 heaping tablespoon ground cumin

1 tablespoon chili powder

1 teaspoon salt

2–3 slices sharp Cheddar cheese

1. Preheat the oven to 350 degrees F. Lightly oil a loaf pan.

2. Heat the oil in a medium-sized skillet over medium-low heat, add the onions and sauté until fragrant, about 8 minutes. Add the garlic and cook for another 2 minutes. Set aside to cool.

3. In a large mixing bowl, use your clean hands to combine all the other ingredients except the cheese slices until well mixed. Add the cooled onions and garlic. Pile the ingredients into the prepared loaf pan. Drape the cheese slices on top.

4. Cook for about 50 minutes or until the internal temperature reaches 155 degrees F. Remove from the oven, let rest for 10 minutes and then slice and serve.

Ricotta Meatball Loaf

Almost every week Jennifer gets a delivery of meat from her local farmer and almost every week that meat becomes meatballs, which are scarfed down by her kids after soccer practice, play rehearsal or what have you, and then tucked into Thermoses the next day for lunch.

One day, when she was stuck with an extra batch and fewer teenage girls at the table than expected, her thoughts turned to meatloaf. Perhaps this was all a matter of thinking of little else but meatloaf for the better part of a year, because really what is meatloaf in many ways but a meatball gone maxi?

But the meatloaf asks less of us in terms of precision and active time. An ill-formed meatball can burn or undercook; a meatloaf just needs its proper beauty rest in the oven. Meatballs must be pushed around a few at a time in the pan or endlessly monitored in the sauce, while meatloaf goes into its pan and leaves you alone until dinner. The meatball is for families; the meatloaf somehow also works better for strangers.

So the loaf was formed, frozen, and cooked at a later date, deliciously. The ricotta cheese gives this loaf a tang, and it is much better on Day Two.

2 teaspoons olive oil

1 small onion, minced

1 pound ground chuck (or dark ground turkey)

1½ cups ricotta cheese

½ cup grated Parmigiano-Reggiano cheese

1 heaping cup panko bread crumbs

1 large egg, lightly beaten

1 tablespoon tomato paste

2 tablespoons chopped fresh basil

2 teaspoons salt

Freshly ground black
    pepper to taste

Ketchup, for the
    glaze (optional)

1. Preheat the oven to
   350 degrees F.
   Line a baking pan with
   aluminum foil or parchment paper.

2. Warm the oil in a medium-sized
   skillet over low heat, add the
   onions and sauté until they are soft,
   roughly 10 minutes. Let them cool in the pan.

3. While the onions are cooking, mix all the remaining ingredients
   (except the ketchup) in a medium-sized bowl. If you are using turkey,

you may need more bread crumbs. The meatloaf batter should form a ball in the hand.

4. Mix in the onions. With clean hands, form a nice large round meatball, and then press it into a loaf shape in the prepared pan. Drizzle the top with ketchup, if desired.

5. Cook for about 45 minutes, until the internal temperature reaches 155 degrees F.

6. Let the loaf rest, uncovered, for 10 minutes. Then slice and serve.

Mashed Potato Meatloaf

Serves 4

There is no side dish quite as meatloaf-friendly as mashed potatoes, so why not put the two together in the ultimate one-dish dinner? (OK, you can also cook some green beans. But why?) The keys to this dish are to avoid over-mixing the potatoes, which would then become gluey in the baking, and to avoid over-filling the meat with your creamy tubers—though if you do, all that means is that they will ooze out over the sides of your loaf and into the pan. In such an event, have a fork ready to go at the pan before the rest of your family and friends catch on.

1 pound Yukon Gold potatoes, peeled and cut into quarters

1 ounce dried shiitake mushrooms

1 cup boiling water

2 teaspoons vegetable oil

3 small shallots, finely chopped

8 tablespoons (1 stick) unsalted butter, at room temperature

¼ cup heavy cream

3 teaspoons salt

1 teaspoon freshly ground black pepper

1 cup rough chunks of white or sourdough bread (crusts removed)

1 pound ground beef chuck

1 pound ground lamb

¾ cup shredded cheese, such as Parmigiano-Reggiano
     or pecorino or a mix

3 tablespoons spicy yellow mustard

1 large egg, lightly beaten

¼ cup ketchup

1. Preheat the oven to 350 degrees F. Line a rimmed baking sheet with aluminum foil.

2. Place the potatoes in a large saucepan; add enough cold water to cover, and bring to a boil over high heat. Then reduce the heat to medium and cook until tender, about 20 minutes.

3. While the potatoes cook, place the dried mushrooms in a bowl, cover them with the 1 cup boiling water, and let them soak for about 20 minutes.

4. Also while the potatoes cook, heat the oil in a medium pan over medium heat and sauté the shallots until soft, about 5 minutes.

5. Transfer the cooked potatoes to a colander and drain; then return them to the pan. Mash the potatoes in the pan until they are light and fluffy. Add the butter, cream, 1 teaspoon of the salt and ½ teaspoon of the pepper. Stir until combined (do not over-mash), and set aside.

6. Drain the mushrooms, reserving the soaking water, and add the bread to that water to soak. Finely chop the mushrooms. Add the mushrooms to the shallots, lower the heat, and cook for another 10 minutes, until soft. Then let cool slightly.

7. Combine the ground beef, ground lamb, cheese, mustard, egg, remaining 2 teaspoons salt and remaining ½ teaspoon pepper in a large bowl. Remove the bread from the water, squeeze out the excess water and shred the bread; add it to the meat mixture. Add the shallots and mushrooms and mix with your clean hands. Place half the mixture on the prepared baking sheet and form it into an 11-by-6-inch loaf. Spread 1½ cups of the mashed potatoes on top of the meat mixture, leaving a 1-inch border all around.

8. Place the remaining meat mixture on top of the potatoes, and form into a loaf, encasing the potato mixture and sealing the edges. Brush with the ketchup. Bake the meatloaf until medium-rare, about 50 minutes; check the center for doneness (155 degrees F is right for medium-rare). Let the loaf rest, uncovered, for 10 minutes; then slice and serve.

SEVEN

Political Postscript

Jenn: We live in a polarized political culture, and yet somehow the loaf unites us. Engage politicians from either party on the subject of meatloaf, and they will wax eloquent about their childhood favorite, or about the one they make themselves. Just as the loaf is the litmus test for so many chefs and home cooks, so it is for members of Congress. House Speaker Paul Ryan makes his venison loaf (page 208) from the deer he kills himself. His San Francisco–based counterpart, Representative Nancy Pelosi, the leader of House Democrats, fashions her family's loaf (page 210) from healthy-ish bison, which she does not kill herself. The salient point is that We The People understand that the identity of this great nation is defined, in part, by its meatloaf ways, and a handful of members of Congress have agreed to share their recipes.

Frank: I second that motion. Is it a motion? Can I vote for cloture? Or will you filibuster me? Sorry, I'm just trying to impress you with my congressional lexicon. One of the odd things about you and me— one of the *many* odd things about you and me—is that our writing and our sensibilities straddle the kitchen and the Capitol, so this chapter seems especially fitting. And, as you say, it shows anew how meatloaf is mirror. Nancy Pelosi's loaf inevitably evokes the West, which is her region. Chuck Schumer's loaf (page 215) has the sort of blunt practicality you'd expect from him. It's like a two-pot dinner, a double entree in one. Please explain it to our readers.

Jenn: There is barbecue chicken, which, for many of us, is, well, a meal. But wait! The chicken surrounds a classic beef loaf, one also infused with barbecue sauce—Kansas City–style sauce, specifically. Like Speaker Ryan, Senator Schumer takes advantage of an ingredient that you won't find in most of our loaves but that is the essence of many traditional recipes: a packet of Lipton onion soup mix. But is it unfair of us to see the senior senator from New York as hinting at the political proclivity for having things both ways?

Frank: If politicians don't have to commit, they don't commit, and Senator Schumer's contribution to this book—I say this with love!— is the commitment-phobe of all loaves. If politicians can please multiple constituencies at once, they do, and Senator Schumer is after the beef-lovers, the pork-lovers, the veal-lovers and the chicken-lovers all at once. I'm surprised he didn't call for shrimp to be sprinkled atop the loaf (seafood-lovers!) along with ribbons of tofu (vegetarians!). All of that said, it's a damned interesting loaf, and I bet no small number of readers will make it.

Jenn: Finally, we have Senator Susan Collins of Maine, who takes a very strong interest in what comes out of her kitchen. While she is at home among a broad array of dishes from around the world, she often refers to her mother's catalogue, developed over the years for their large family. Her loaf (page 213) involves bell peppers and gets a special zip from horseradish and dry mustard. We were very proud that we were able to perfectly emulate the loaf of her youth in our own kitchens, which we can state with confidence because when we brought her a slice to taste, she was so enamored with it that she wished to discuss it for a full thirty minutes. This did not amuse her staff, who were trying to usher her off to give a speech.

Frank: This is why we and so many other Americans respect Senator Collins so much. She has priorities. She has *values*. She knows what's important, and when standing at a fork in the road, with oratory in one direction and ground meat in the other, she heads without hesitation toward the loaf.

Oh, Deer, Speaker Paul Ryan's Loaf

The only topic that animates House Speaker Paul Ryan more than the earned income tax credit and its potential adjustments in the context of tax reform is the killing of deer. He's such an avid hunter that he grows a beard during deer season, talks endlessly about his wilderness escapades (which usually involve bows and arrows) and even told some of his colleagues that he was solo in a deer blind when he made the ultimate decision to run for Speaker.

The Speaker grinds his own meat, of course, employing a power grinder during hunting season. From that he makes his own venison meatloaf, which his family loves to devour. (He cooks, his wife does the dishes, per their marital accord.)

Apart from its protein, this loaf is a very traditional one, largely by dint of its onion soup mix, commercial bread crumbs and, of course, ketchup. Venison is lean, so the ground beef paired with it in this recipe should not be. And the beef is important: It mellows the gaminess of the venison. Don't skimp on the ketchup, which gives this fairly dense loaf a pivotal zing.

"Ain't no way Ryan is doing a P90X workout after eating this!" noted one taster.

1 tablespoon olive oil

1 medium-sized onion, finely chopped

1 pound ground venison

½ pound fatty ground beef, preferably not more than 70 percent lean

1 envelope Lipton Recipe Secrets onion soup mix

1 tablespoon Worcestershire sauce

½ cup Progresso Italian-style bread crumbs

1 large egg, lightly beaten

¼ cup ketchup

1. Preheat the oven to 350 degrees F. Line a baking pan with aluminum foil, or, alternatively, get out your nonstick loaf pan.

2. Warm the oil in a medium-sized skillet over low heat, add the onions and sauté until soft, about 10 minutes. Let cool slightly.

3. Combine the meats, onion soup mix, Worcestershire, bread crumbs and egg in a large bowl and mix gently with your clean hands until combined. Add the cooled onions and knead them into the mixture until just incorporated.

4. Form the mixture into a loaf in the prepared baking pan, or gently press it into the loaf pan, and glaze the top with the ketchup. Bake until the internal temperature reaches 160 degrees F, about 65 minutes.

5. Let the loaf rest, uncovered, for 10 minutes before slicing and serving.

Nancy Pelosi's Italian-Style Bison Loaf

Serves 6

This recipe was designed in collaboration with the House Democratic Minority Leader's six-year-old granddaughter, Bella, one of the new generation of precocious chefs. It highlights the grassy qualities of the bison and the subtle elegance of the veal, both lean meats. The fresh rosemary is a nod to Pelosi's Italian heritage, of which she is very proud, as is the interesting addition of ciabatta chunks rather than seasoned bread crumbs.

But things get mischievous with the appearance of cumin, a spice that tends to be associated with other continents, and with a heat hit courtesy of the cayenne. This loaf sets up best in a nonstick loaf pan, but you should rest a rimmed baking sheet on the oven shelf beneath the pan to catch any fat that might otherwise drip onto your oven floor, thus setting off a smoke detector that could possibly spark a fight with your spouse about whose turn it is to clean the oven and why am I the only one who folds laundry around here. Ahem.

The Minority Leader suggests you enjoy this with a Caesar salad freshly prepared at the table. For the best recipe, she says, contact her husband, Paul Pelosi.

1 tablespoon olive oil, plus extra for greasing the loaf pan

1 medium-sized onion, chopped

½ loaf ciabatta bread, cut into large pieces (about 3 cups)

2½ cups whole milk

1 pound ground bison

1 pound ground veal

½ cup grated Parmigiano-Reggiano cheese, plus ⅓ cup for
    sprinkling on top

½ cup grated Romano cheese

2 tablespoons Worcestershire sauce

1 tablespoon sea salt

2 teaspoons ground cumin

1 teaspoon cayenne pepper

1 teaspoon freshly ground black pepper

1 tablespoon plus 1 teaspoon finely chopped fresh rosemary leaves

1 tablespoon plus 1 teaspoon finely chopped fresh cilantro leaves

2 eggs, beaten

1. Preheat the oven to 375 degrees F. Grease a (preferably nonstick) loaf pan with olive oil.

2. Heat the olive oil in a medium-sized skillet over medium heat, add the onions and sauté until soft, about 7 minutes. Set aside to cool.

3. While the onions are cooking, soak the ciabatta chunks in the milk in a bowl.

4. Mix the bison and veal in a large bowl, using your clean hands. Add the ½ cup each of Parmesan and Romano, the Worcestershire, the

spices and the 1 tablespoon each of rosemary and cilantro. In a small bowl, mix together the remaining Parmesan and herbs; set this aside.

5. Remove the pieces of bread from the milk, drain them and then rip them into smaller pieces; then mix the bread, eggs and cooled onions into the meat mixture. Carefully press the mixture into the prepared loaf pan.

6. Sprinkle the reserved mixture of cheese and herbs over the top of the loaf.

7. Bake until a meat thermometer reads 175 degrees F at the center of the loaf, roughly 1 hour 15 minutes.

8. Remove the meatloaf from the oven and let it rest for 5 minutes before slicing and serving.

Senator Susan Collins's Bipartisan Loaf

Serves 6

Senator Susan Collins of Maine may be best known for her willingness to cooperate with colleagues across the aisle and for her expertise on appropriations, but her non-political passion is all things food. She runs a weekly lunch group with her fellow Republicans, in which each member shows off his or her home-state specialty. She spends every weekend in front of the stove or oven, cooking up treats for her husband.

Among his favorites is the meatloaf created by her mother, Pat. It has a few special twists: pungent dry mustard, horseradish and a topping of barbecue sauce rather than ketchup. "I grew up in a large family with five brothers and sisters," the senator told us. "The six of us all had very different food preferences, but on one thing we were unanimous: We all loved my mother's meatloaf."

2 teaspoons olive oil

3/4 cup minced onion

2 large eggs

2 pounds ground chuck

2 cups fresh bread crumbs

¼ cup minced green bell peppers

2 tablespoons prepared
    horseradish

2 tablespoons dry mustard

¼ cup whole milk

¾ cup barbecue sauce

1 slice bacon

1. Preheat the oven to 400 degrees F. Line a baking sheet or a large baking pan with parchment paper. (This loaf can also be made in a lightly oiled loaf pan, to keep it strictly Pat Collins correct.)

2. Warm the olive oil in a small skillet over low heat, add the onions and sauté until they are soft and fragrant, about 7 minutes. Set aside.

3. In a large bowl, beat the eggs lightly with a fork. Mix in the beef and then the bread crumbs, (slightly cooled) onions and bell peppers. Add the horseradish, dry mustard, milk and ¼ cup of the barbecue sauce and lightly combine with your clean hands until just mixed. Shape the mixture into a loaf on the baking sheet or pack it gently into a loaf pan.

4. Place the bacon slice lengthwise on top, and then spread the remaining ½ cup barbecue sauce over the loaf.

5. Bake for roughly 50 minutes, until the internal temperature reaches about 150 degrees F. Let the loaf rest, uncovered, for 10 minutes, then slice and serve.

Senator Chuck Schumer's Omnibus Loaf

As a powerful United States senator and longtime leader of the Democratic Party, Senator Schumer often finds himself going out for dinner, preferably at his favorite hole-in-the-wall Chinese restaurant near Capitol Hill. But when he's at home in Brooklyn, Schumer and his wife, Iris, often cook.

In the winter months, they sometimes turn to this rather oddball recipe concocted by the senator's homemaker mother, Selma. You know surf 'n' turf? Well, this beef-plus-poultry combo could be called chuck 'n' cluck. It's a fairly standard meatloaf recipe surrounded by—wait for it!—barbecued chicken.

Fancy it isn't: You can make the entire thing with ingredients culled from your ShopRite cart. But consoling, yes, which politicians often need. The chicken absorbs some of the fat and thus the flavors of the meat, especially the pork, while the loaf itself reflects the barbecue essence of the chicken.

If you don't have time to marinate the chicken pieces for an hour, a half hour will be okay. You also may skip the glaze if you want to reduce the smoky sweetness of the dish.

Hibernate after eating.

1 chicken, cut up into 8 pieces

1 tablespoon plus 1 teaspoon kosher salt

2¾ cups Masterpiece Kansas City Classic barbecue sauce
   (roughly 1 28-ounce bottle)

1 pound ground beef

½ pound ground pork

½ pound ground veal

2 eggs, lightly beaten

1 envelope Lipton Recipe Secrets onion soup mix

½ cup bread crumbs

1 teaspoon garlic powder

1 teaspoon dried oregano

1 teaspoon freshly ground black pepper

1. Season the chicken pieces with the 1 tablespoon kosher salt, place them in a large bowl and cover with 2 cups of the barbecue sauce. Marinate for 1 hour at room temperature.

2. When the chicken is nearly done marinating, preheat the oven to 350 degrees F. Line a large baking dish with aluminum foil.

3. In a large bowl, combine the ground meats, eggs, onion soup mix, bread crumbs, garlic powder, oregano, pepper and remaining 1 teaspoon salt (no more—there is a lot of sodium in the soup mix); mix with your clean hands. Add ½ cup of the remaining barbecue sauce.

4. In the prepared baking dish, mold the loaf into an oval shape and brush it with the last ¼ cup of barbecue sauce. (This last step is optional as there is plenty of sauce in the meatloaf already.)

5. Arrange the chicken pieces around the meatloaf, discarding any marinade remaining in the bowl. Bake until the internal temperature of the loaf reaches 160 degrees F, about 1 hour 15 minutes. Let the loaf rest (along with the chicken) for 10 minutes, then slice and serve.

Sides

Frank: To be utterly frank, Jenn, this chapter feels to me like a broken promise. A betrayal. A surrender. We set out to do an all-meatloaf cookbook—bravely venturing where few had ventured before!—and here we are moving *beyond* meatloaf into a realm without beef, without pork, without lamb, without *loaf*. We're culinary evangelists whose religion is meatloaf, so refresh my memory and justify this chapter: Why are we straying to a different god? How is this not heresy?

Jenn: You are borrowing trouble where none exists and failing to anticipate the pleasure from the deviant. The fact is, people are going to have other people in their homes, and they will be serving them meatloaf. Picnics are going to happen. Sack lunches shall be packed. A person needs a side dish. Traditionally with meatloaf, that has meant one of two accomplices: mashed potatoes or green beans. We are offering fantastic versions of both here—our friend Helene's divine mashed potatoes (page 222), which she serves each year at her IKEA meatball party, and green beans (page 230) cooked in a manner that best accompanies some of our loaves from around the world.

Frank: We should let our readers know that "Helene" is none other than Helene Cooper, a globe-trotting *New York Times* correspondent, which I mention not to drop names but to illustrate a point: IKEA meatball fans are many and sophisticated. (That's why the IKEA meatball inspired one of our meat*loaves* in an earlier chapter.) Anyway, yes, yes, you're right: Man (and woman) cannot live on loaf alone, and some roughage and starch are called for. Some macaroni and cheese, for example. Thanks to the chef (and *Top Chef* competitor) Garret Fleming, we have a sublime one (page 226).

Jenn: Speaking of chefs, a few others have come through with some counterintuitive veggie sides for our loaves. The Brussels sprouts (page 240) from Sam Molavi, the chef at Compass Rose in Washington, D.C., take approximately five minutes to put together and go especially well with our Asian-inspired dishes. Ditto for Bobby Flay's superb shiitake mushroom salad (page 242), which, should it be sitting on your plate during your work lunch, will make your colleagues deeply jealous.

Frank: I realize only as we discuss this how much this chapter, despite my reservations, excites me. Just as I've never had macaroni and cheese I've liked better than the one here, I'm mad for this potato salad (page 234), which has what any proper potato salad should: a backstory. My mother, whose meatloaf appears in this book, had a potato salad we all adored. It went light on the vinegar and the mustard. It didn't get carried away with sweet pickles. The *potato* was front and center, where it belongs. She never wrote the recipe down. So over the years, my sister, Adelle, experimented, trying to figure it out and come up with something identical. That's this recipe: not an intricate one, not a fancy one, just a really, really satisfying one that, for me, is packed with as many memories as calories.

Jenn: Come for the potato salad, stay for the carrots. For fun with veggies, I once again dug into the archives of Food52.com, where I had a home cooking blog for years and where I discovered some of the stars of my weeknight menu rotation. Among them are the Moroccan carrots (page 238), which are sweetly seasoned with North African spices and honey. I've made these carrots for something like a hundred dinner parties, including one where my guests insisted upon discussing the economic history of Southern railways (because I live in Washington, D.C.) and I was *so happy* to have these carrots to distract me. Also in this chapter, Amanda Hesser, who co-founded Food52, keeps things healthy and textural with her go-to couscous (page 232). And if you are making meatloaf in winter, which is likely, the fennel salad here (page 224) gives you a tiny sliver of spring on the plate, along with seasonal salad veggies. Finally, my gentleman caller recently corrected my lifelong habit of steaming broccoli by showing me that it is just as fast and three hundred times more delicious to roast it in the oven (page 236). Salt and pepper alone will do, but adding the smoked paprika makes it special enough for guests. Or just your special someone.

Frank: What we've done with these recipes, I realize, isn't to betray meatloaf. We've made it more possible for a reader to follow us into the land of loaf by mapping out the rest of the meal by putting lakes beside the meatloaf mountains, rivers through the meatloaf valleys. OK, I think I've clubbed the topography metaphor to death. And I think it's time for us to zip our lips and for readers to fire up their stoves.

Helene's Extremely Delicious Mashed Potatoes

Our friend Helene Cooper leans spicy. A native of Liberia, she likes her food with a side of heat, lacing her stews with chiles and decorating her vegetables with peppers as others would do with poppy seeds. A great lover of mashed potatoes, Helene is known for throwing a large handful of habaneros into her mash, which has become famous among her relatives as an expected Christmas dinner side dish.

But a week later, when Helene has her annual meatball party, she tames her inner heat meter with this super-creamy, slightly tangy, overall addictive mash with sour cream. No need to peel your Yukon potatoes; the skins more or less melt when cooked. If it looks dry at all as you mix, add more cream.

3 pounds Yukon Gold potatoes, quartered (no need to peel)

½ cup whole milk

½ cup heavy cream

8 tablespoons (1 stick) unsalted butter

1 cup sour cream

Salt and freshly ground black pepper to taste

1. Bring a large pot of salted water to a boil, add the potatoes, and boil for 15 to 20 minutes, until fork-tender. Drain, and let them cool slightly.

2. While the potatoes are cooling, heat the milk, cream and butter all together in a microwave-safe measuring cup in the microwave for 45 seconds or until the butter has melted.

3. Put the potatoes in a large bowl, and use a hand masher to mash them (you can use an electric hand mixer, but on a low speed and watch out for over-mixing as it will turn the potatoes gummy). Add the sour cream and keep mashing. Then add the hot milk-cream-butter mixture a little at a time, and keep mashing. If the potatoes seem too dry, add more hot milk.

4. Season with salt and pepper and serve.

Winter Salad of Fennel, Celery Root, Lemon, and Pecorino

Food blogger Cristina Sciarra shared this salad with Food52.com, and we find it a real winner. It is a great accompaniment to meatloaf, thanks to its crunchy and fresh-from-the-garden qualities, even though everything in it is available all winter.

We especially love the bite of the fennel mixed with the subtle kiss of the celery root, which you should really get someone else to cut for you because, after all, you made the meatloaf! Cristina uses a mandoline to cut all three vegetables and the pecorino, but it is okay if you don't have that tool. Just make sure you slice everything nice and thin.

1 small bulb celery root

1 large fennel bulb

1 small red onion

1 large lemon, cut in half (or 5 tablespoons fresh lemon juice)

½ cup chopped fresh parsley

Heaping ½ cup thinly sliced pecorino cheese (we used a mandoline,

but you can also do this by hand)

¼ teaspoon crunchy sea salt

25 turns of a pepper mill

3 tablespoons raw pumpkin seeds

7 tablespoons good-quality olive oil

1. First, prepare the vegetables: Start by peeling the celery root. If you have a mandoline with a julienne blade, use that to slice the peeled celery root. Otherwise, do it by hand, aiming for ⅛-inch-thick matchsticks. Next, trim the fennel so that just the bulb remains. (If there are fronds attached, you can chop and add them to the salad.) Cut off the heel of the bulb, and then slice the bulb in half lengthwise. On a mandoline or by hand, slice each half crosswise, even thinner than the celery root. Cut the red onion in half lengthwise and slice it into wispy half-moons. Toss the vegetables into a large mixing bowl.

fennel

2. Squeeze the lemon juice from the halves into the mixing bowl, and with your clean hands, mix the juice evenly into the vegetables. Add the parsley and the pecorino. Sprinkle the salt, pepper, pumpkin seeds and olive oil over the ingredients and use your hands (or tongs) to mix the salad evenly. Divide the salad among individual plates; enjoy.

Garret Fleming's Macaroni and Cheese

I t's possible that you know Garret Fleming from *Top Chef: California*, the hit TV show's thirteenth season, which began airing in the fall of 2015. Or it's possible that you know him because you've eaten at his Washington, D.C., restaurant Barrel, where the full-flavored, go-for-broke food reflects his Southern heritage. (He grew up and first worked in Charleston, S.C.)

But once you try this recipe, it's the way you'll know, revere and remember him forevermore.

This is a somewhat involved execution of a classic dish. It's also an expensive production, using an array of cheeses with price points well above Velveeta's. But all of that pays off. We cursed the cost and labor while doing the shopping and cooking, then woke the next morning with an itch to make it again soon. It's that special.

GREMOLATA CRUMB

4 tablespoons (½ stick) salted butter

1 tablespoon minced garlic

2 teaspoons minced fresh thyme

1½ teaspoons grated lemon zest

1½ cups panko bread crumbs

2 tablespoons minced fresh parsley

½ teaspoon freshly ground black pepper

2 teaspoons salt

MACARONI AND CHEESE

1 pound (1 box) elbow macaroni, rigatoni, gemelli, cavatappi
   or other favorite dry pasta

1 quart heavy cream

2 sprigs fresh thyme

¼ cup Dijon mustard

1 cup grated Fontal or Fontina Valle d'Aosta cheese

½ cup crumbled goat cheese

½ cup grated aged Parmigiano-Reggiano cheese

⅔ cup grated Gruyère or Comté cheese

1 large egg

1–2 teaspoons salt

¼ teaspoon freshly grated nutmeg (use a Microplane grater)

1 cup grated Danish fontina

FOR THE GREMOLATA CRUMB

1. In a large sauté pan, melt the butter over low heat.

2. Add the garlic and cook for 1 minute.

3. Add the thyme, lemon zest and bread crumbs, and cook, stirring constantly, for 7 to 12 minutes, until the mixture is golden brown and aromatic.

4. Add the parsley, pepper and salt, give it a final stir, and then quickly remove the pan from the burner and place on a baking rack to cool.

FOR THE MACARONI AND CHEESE

1. Preheat the oven to 400 degrees F.

2. On the stovetop, bring a large pot of salted water to a boil.

3. Add the pasta and cook for 1 to 2 minutes less than you usually would, draining it well at the end to make sure it's dry; then transfer three-quarters of the pasta to a large mixing bowl. Reserve the rest.

4. In a medium-sized saucepan over medium-high heat, bring the cream to a simmer, stirring occasionally so it doesn't burn, and add the thyme sprigs.

5. Lower the heat slightly and reduce the cream for 10 minutes, keeping an eye on it to make sure it doesn't boil over.

6. Remove the thyme, add the Dijon mustard, and bring the cream to a simmer again.

7. Add the Fontal, goat cheese, Parmesan and Gruyère, and cook for just a few minutes, stirring occasionally, until they've melted. Remove from the heat.

8. Add the cream-and-cheese mixture, along with the egg, salt and nutmeg, to the pasta bowl and mix well. The resulting mixture should

be wet but not soupy; stir in some of the reserved pasta if you need to. Discard any remaing pasta.

9. Transfer the mixture to a casserole dish that's large enough to fit all the pasta and sauce.

10. Sprinkle the Danish fontina over the top of the mixture, put the casserole in the oven and bake for about 10 minutes, or until the cheese has melted completely and the sauce is bubbling at the sides.

11. Remove from the oven and let rest, uncovered, for 1 minute; then sprinkle the Gremolata Crumb on top and serve.

Quick and Easy Super-Snappy Green Beans

Serves 6

There is something very natural about the marriage of green beans and meatloaf, though I cannot put my finger on the genesis of their courtship. Somehow the sloppy green bean casserole, the one that uses the fried onions in a can and is a staple on many Easter dinner tables, feels like the progenitor of all things green bean and meat.

A healthier and fresher option, one more exciting than simply steamed beans, rests in partially cooking them on the stove, then finishing them in a pan with some lemon zest and juice, to add some zing. The sesame seeds are optional, but they do add an elegant touch.

1 tablespoon sesame seeds (optional)

1 tablespoon kosher salt

1 pound green beans, trimmed

2 tablespoons olive oil

1 tablespoon grated lemon zest

1 tablespoon fresh lemon juice

Salt and freshly ground black pepper to taste

1. If you are using them, toast the sesame seeds on an ungreased baking sheet in a 350-degree F oven until lightly browned—about 8 minutes. Set aside to cool.

2. Meanwhile, fill a large bowl with ice water and set it near the stove.

3. Fill a large pot with water and add the 1 tablespoon of salt. Bring the water to a rolling boil, drop in the green beans and then lower the heat. Cook just until the beans are bright green, about 2 minutes; then transfer them to the bowl of ice water to stop the cooking. Drain and pat dry.

4. In a large skillet over medium-high heat, heat the oil until it is shimmering. Add the beans, tossing so each gets coated with oil, and sauté until cooked through, about 3 minutes. (You may need to do this in batches.) Transfer the beans to a large serving bowl.

5. Toss the beans with the lemon zest, lemon juice, sesame seeds if using and salt and pepper. Serve while hot or at room temperature.

Amanda Hesser's Couscous with Celery, Parsley and Red Wine Vinegar

Serves 4

There are not many contemporary food folks with the cred of Amanda Hesser, a former *New York Times* scribe who broke out on her own in the middle of a tech-bubble disaster to bravely start Food52.com, the innovative leader in crowdsourced recipe sites. While we have gotten many a delicious meal off Food52.com over the past decade, we still love to go to Amanda's original recipes, which never fail us when someone shows up for dinner on the fly in search of something delicious. This does actually happen.

This recipe was developed with her husband, a.k.a. Mr. Latte, and appears in her memoir of their courtship, *Cooking for Mr. Latte*. We think it's a great meatloaf companion, in lieu of the traditional potatoes.

2 cups beef broth

1 cup couscous

5 tender inner stalks celery, finely chopped

4 large sprigs fresh parsley, stemmed and finely chopped

¼ cup safflower oil

2 tablespoons red wine vinegar

Sea salt and freshly ground black pepper to taste

1. In a small saucepan, bring the beef broth to a boil. Place the couscous in a medium-sized heatproof serving bowl. Pour the boiling broth over the couscous, cover with a lid or plastic wrap, and let stand for 5 minutes.

2. Scatter the celery and parsley over the couscous. Sprinkle with the oil and vinegar, and stir until well mixed. Season with salt and pepper.

3. Let sit for another 5 minutes; then taste and adjust the seasoning if needed before serving.

Good Old Midwestern Potato Salad

Meatloaf goes well with all manner of potatoes, but in the summer, we prefer them in salad form. While there are as many ways to make potato salad as there are ways to blow your Powerball winnings, we like ours with a strong hint of mustard and mayonnaise both, and with some tang, provided here by the sour cream and pickles.

This potato salad is best when it is made in advance, preferably one day ahead.

4 large Red Bliss or Yukon Gold potatoes (do not peel but scrub
   them clean)

3 hard-boiled eggs, finely chopped

2–3 scallions (white parts), finely chopped

2 tablespoons sweet pickle relish

¾ cup mayonnaise (decrease or increase to your preferred
   creaminess)

¼ cup sour cream

1 rounded teaspoon prepared yellow mustard

Salt and freshly ground black pepper to taste

Celery seeds to taste

1. Fill a large pot with cold water and add the potatoes right away. Liberally salt the water and bring it to a boil with the immersed potatoes and cook them until they are soft, about 20 minutes. Drain, and let them cool until you can handle them. Then peel and cut them into bite-sized chunks.

2. Using a large spoon, mix the remaining ingredients together well in a large bowl. Then fold the potatoes into the mixture; you can add more mayo at this time if you prefer a creamier salad. Chill, covered, for one hour before serving

Jonathan's Roasted Broccoli

Serves 4

We do many things with broccoli—steam, fry, dump it in casseroles—but we rarely think to roast it. This is a very sad mistake because unlike root veggies and tubers, broccoli florets roast very quickly and at a low temperature to boot.

The earthy, almost smoky flavor is a revelation, and salt and oil will do you just fine toward that end, but a dash of smoked paprika raises the bar. Served with meatloaf, this dish is practically spa-like.

1 pound broccoli, trimmed to
   florets with most stem
   removed

¼ cup olive oil

1 tablespoon kosher
   salt

½ teaspoon smoked
   paprika

1. Preheat the oven to 325 degrees F. Line a baking sheet with aluminum foil.

2. Spread the broccoli across the prepared baking sheet, and drizzle the olive oil over the florets, followed by the salt and paprika.

3. Bake until slightly soft, about 15 minutes. Serve.

"It's Maaaa-gic!" Moroccan Carrots

Serves 4

Another winner from our pals at Food52.com, specifically Virginia Kellner. It's a recipe so delicious and simple that we've served these carrots over and over and even doubled the amount for Thanksgiving. What you are doing is cutting, simmering, adding some more stuff and simmering some more. You can't really overcook this if you keep your heat low, and it can be made ahead of time, as it is lovely at room temperature.

Virginia calls for "skinny carrots" but the real key is to use nice, delicious carrots of any size, cut into uniform pieces. Please watch your spices and garlic carefully as you heat them—burning will ruin the dish. When you combine said spices, carrots, tomatoes and chickpeas all together, you will probably need a bit of water (or if you prefer, stock) to keep it from scorching, but not much.

Be sure to keep that heat low so if you leave it on a bit too long, no calamity will occur.

1 pound skinny carrots, peeled and cut into cubes

1 teaspoon olive oil

238

1 teaspoon ground cinnamon

1 teaspoon grated nutmeg

1 teaspoon ground cumin

1 teaspoon paprika

1 teaspoon caraway seeds

½ teaspoon ground ginger

2 cloves garlic, smashed

1 14.5-ounce can chopped tomatoes, juice and all

1 14.5-ounce can chickpeas, drained well

1 tablespoon honey or other sweetener

¼ cup chopped fresh cilantro (optional)

1. Bring a saucepan of salted water to a boil, add the carrots and cook until tender, 5 to 7 minutes (longer if you cut into large pieces).

2. Meanwhile, heat the oil in a medium saucepan and add all the spices and the garlic; cook, stirring, over medium-low heat for about three minutes, until the kitchen starts to smell like Rabat or Marrakesh.

3. Drain the carrots and stir them into the spices along with the tomatoes, chickpeas and honey. Simmer for about 15 minutes, adding water if needed. Then stir in the cilantro, if using, and serve.

Sam Molavi's Wow Brussels Sprouts

This recipe comes to us courtesy of Sam Molavi, the chef at the Washington, D.C., restaurant Compass Rose Bar & Kitchen, which specializes in street food from around the world. While its hottest seller is *khachapuri*, the classic cheese-filled bread served in the Republic of Georgia, the restaurant also regularly sells out of his divine Brussels sprouts, which employ a mix of global flavors.

These are flash-fried—a revelation in Brussels sprouts cooking—so it is important to keep your oil at 325 degrees F. The easiest way to do this is with a candy thermometer, although you can use a popcorn kernel, which pops at somewhere between 325 and 350 degrees F, to test the oil. Please use extreme caution when you put these fellas in the oil, as splatter is inevitable.

We love that this is all mixed up at the end in a large bowl, which we licked clean, though we concede that this was unattractive of us.

¼ cup crumbled feta cheese

2 tablespoons minced smoked ham

¼ cup soy sauce (whiskey barrel–aged if you can find it)

1 tablespoon white sesame seeds, toasted (see instructions on page

230, Quick and Easy Super-Snappy Green Beans)

1 tablespoon black sesame seeds, toasted

¼ cup diced scallions (white and light green parts)

1 quart canola oil

2 cups quartered and trimmed Brussels sprouts

1. Mix the feta, ham, soy sauce, sesame seeds and scallions together in a medium-sized serving bowl set near the stove.

2. Heat the canola oil to 325 degrees F in a large, wide, straight-sided frying pan.

3. Carefully and gently add the Brussels sprouts to the hot oil (the oil may splatter).

4. Fry the sprouts for approximately 1 minute; if you are doing this in batches, check the oil temperature between batches as it may cool a bit when you remove a batch.

5. Use a strainer to transfer the Brussels sprouts to the bowl containing the other ingredients. You do not need salt, as the feta and soy have plenty of it! Toss and serve.

Bobby Flay's Shiitake Mushroom Salad

Serves 4

Bobby Flay generously concocted this salad—which of course is not a salad in the traditional sense, as it does not involve a single leafy green—to accompany his spicy Korean-Style Meatloaf (page 61). We think it goes well with any of the meatloaves (and the meatless loaves, too) that feature Asian seasonings or that can stand up to them. If you want more of the buttery flavor of the shiitakes, cut the amount of dressing a bit.

3 tablespoons canola oil

5 large fresh shiitake mushrooms, stemmed, caps coarsely chopped

Kosher salt and freshly ground black pepper to taste

2 large scallions (dark green and pale green parts), thinly sliced

1 tablespoon low-sodium soy sauce

Finely grated zest and juice of 1 lime

1 teaspoon toasted sesame oil

¼ cup finely chopped fresh cilantro leaves

1. Heat the oil in a large sauté pan over high heat until it begins to shimmer. Add the mushrooms and cook, stirring occasionally, until they are golden brown, about 10 minutes. Season with salt and pepper.

2. Transfer the mushrooms to a bowl. Add the scallions, soy sauce, lime zest and juice, sesame oil and cilantro and mix to combine. Serve.

Acknowledgments

I t almost goes without saying that we're hugely appreciative of the chefs and cooks who contributed recipes, but we'd like to say it nonetheless and to direct you back to the "Contributors" pages, where most of them are identified and where their praises are sung, though not with a volume or at a length commensurate with their generosity and our gratitude. Thanks to all of them, with a special thanks to Cathy Barrow, Melissa Clark and Amanda Hesser, who additionally provided endless advice, technical tips (who knew there was such a variety in the sizes of duck breasts?) and moral support.

The list of friends, relatives and colleagues who fielded loaf-related questions, listened to loaf-related complaints, doled out loaf-related sympathy, made loaf-related suggestions, served as test subjects or shadowed our efforts in the kitchen to help us clarify and refine our recipes is epic. It includes, but is by no means limited to: Esther Fein, Anne Kornblut, Paul Volpe, Lisa Kelly, Josh Isay, Elisabeth Bumiller, Abby Goodnough, Alessandra Stanley, Louis Linfield, Louise Grunwald, a whole bunch of Brunis (Lisa, Adelle, Harry, Sylvia, Mario, Carolyn and Frank Sr.), Russ

Schriefer, Noah Remnick, Rachel Shorey, Nick Fandos, Scott Shane, Alicia Parlapiano, Jill Agostino, Ian Fisher, David Firestone, Nick Corasaniti, Jeremy Bowers, Maya Rao, Nate Sawtell, Laura Evans, Samir Abu-Khadra, Wendy Nevett Bazil, Linda Rittelmann, Helene Cooper, Mark Mazetti, Carl Hulse, Antonia Ferrier, Joel Seidman and Andrew Ginsburg.

Frank would like to express gratitude in particular to his longtime partner, Tom Nickolas, whose appetite is always primed, whose meatloaf tastes are ecumenical and whose quickness to reach for seconds and even thirds is the kind of thing that makes cooking so worthwhile, life so sweet and a lunch of leftovers so apocryphal, at least in their apartment.

Jennifer would like to thank her adored children, Hannah and Sadie Wyatt, who tried very, very hard not to say "Meatloaf again?!" too often; Jonathan Weisman, who tasted and copyedited for months on end; and his children, Hannah and Alissa Weisman, who have actually asked for more meatloaf again soon, please.

This book would not exist without the efforts and sage counsel of the incredible team at Grand Central Publishing—including Deb Futter, Jamie Raab, Ben Greenberg, Maddie Caldwell, Elizabeth Kulhanek, Yasmin Mathew and Jimmy Franco—and the support of our agents, Alia Habib, Lisa Bankoff and Amanda Urban.

Index

About the Authors

Frank Bruni is the author of three bestselling books and an op-ed columnist for the *New York Times*. Prior, he worked as the newspaper's Rome bureau chief, White House correspondent and chief restaurant critic.

Jennifer Steinhauer is a veteran *New York Times* correspondent, passionate home chef and the author of the bestselling cookbook *Treat Yourself* as well as the novel *Beverly Hills Adjacent* with Jessica Hendra.